WOMEN,
ANGER & DEPRESSION

STRATEGIES FOR
SELF-EMPOWERMENT

Lois P. Frankel, Ph.D.

Health Communications, Inc.
Deerfield Beach, Florida

Lois P. Frankel, Ph.D.
The Frankel & Fox Group
Los Angeles, California

Library of Congress Cataloging-in-Publication Data

Frankel, Lois P.
    Women, anger, and depression: strategies for self-empow-
erment/by Lois P. Frankel.
    p.   cm.
    ISBN 1-55874-161-5
    1. Depression, Mental. 2. Anger — Health aspects. 3.
Women — Mental health. I. Title.
RC537.F675 1991   91-6824
616.85′27′082—dc20   CIP

©1992 Lois P. Frankel
ISBN 1-55874-161-5

Publisher: Health Communications, Inc.
               3201 S.W. 15th Street
               Deerfield Beach, Florida 33442-8190

Cover design by Iris T. Slones

ACKNOWLEDGMENTS

The thoughts, comments and experiences of many people went into the writing of this book. While it is impossible to thank everyone, I would like to make special mention of several individuals, beginning with my clients from whom I continue to learn and who provided me with much of the insight necessary to write this book. I also want to thank Drs. Karen Otazo, Betty Mathis, Frank Fox, Joyce Miller and Barbara Stephens for their assistance, both personal and professional. I cannot possibly express enough thanks to my own support network, Dorothy Potts, Sandra Rodriguez and Shirley Trissler, for their unfailing belief in me and my vision of this project. The staff at Health Communications, including Teri Miller, Lisa Moro and Marie Stilkind is thanked for answering my myriad of questions from pre-submission through publication. Last, but not least, I thank my mother, Sonia, for instilling in me through her own actions the notion that I am as powerful as I choose to be.

Names and characteristics pertaining to the clients described in this work have been significantly altered to preserve confidentiality and the identity of each person.

CONTENTS

INTRODUCTION

Congratulations! Your choosing to read this book is the next step in the journey that you have been on for a long time . . . your entire life. For that is how you can look at the process of growth and self-improvement. It is a journey without a road map. It takes us to unknown and often hidden places. As you begin to shed light on some of these places, you may find things you don't like about yourself or others. As you read this book, you may find ideas that are helpful in moving from one place to another in your development. Or you may want to toss this book out the window. For these reasons I ask you to consider three things before you begin reading.

First, I ask that you remain open and willing to be diverted down paths that may have been previously unexplored for you. So often I find that when new ideas are presented, we often dismiss them if there is what psychologists call *cognitive dissonance*. Since the idea or concept is inconsistent with what we believe to be true, this creates a kind of mental friction. To maintain orderliness in our world, we may want to move away from the new idea or concept quickly. If you find yourself uncomfortable, it may be that there is something here for you to learn. If after giving it some thought, you still find the new concept doesn't feel right, then toss it out.

Second, don't beat yourself up over things that you think should have been obvious. Women are experts at flagellating themselves for things they think they should have known. I often hear clients say, "I must really be stupid not to have known this." You can't know what you haven't been taught and healthy anger in particular is one thing most women are not familiar with. In fact, they are given messages which suggest healthy anger is a contradiction in terms.

Finally, be kind to yourself along this journey. If you grew up in a home where there was no model for kindness, this last request may be more difficult than it appears. Ask yourself if it was acceptable for you to make mistakes or simply not know something. Or was being perfect and "all-knowing" a prerequisite of your family? This can be a subtle family behavior. There may have been no verbal messages to this effect, but non-verbal messages may have made it clear that there was little room for error. I often tell clients who came from homes like this that one lesson of therapy is to learn to treat yourself better than anyone else ever did. You no longer have to repeat patterns of behavior you learned from your parents, grandparents, teachers or other authority figures. You are now the only authority on your life (contrary to what others would have you believe). As a friend once explained her own therapy, "I'm learning to re-write the script."

The fact that you want to know more about the relationship between anger and depression tells me that you are ready to move from a place of despair and toward a place of fulfillment and control. In a workshop I recently did on this topic I asked the group, "What is control?" One woman thought about it, raised her hand and summed the answer up perfectly: "Being in control means knowing that no matter what happens, I can handle the cards life deals me."

I often hear people say that fulfillment is a dream and something just beyond their grasp. For some, fulfillment has more to do with helping others reach their dreams and less to do with reaching their own. You may be one of those who have come to believe this is just your lot in life or the way things are supposed to be. *Stop.* The fact is that you have the right to be fulfilled, you have the right to realize your dreams and your achievements are limited only by you. Until you believe that, you cannot expect to move from where you now stand to where you would like to be. I would like to think that this book will help you along this journey.

Let me take a moment to tell you what this book is not. It is not a research project which will show with statistical accuracy that depression in women is a function of anger. It is not even designed to convince every woman who reads it that unexpressed anger is the basis for *her* depression and related symptoms. You are not asked to buy into anything that doesn't feel right to you. As I have told my clients many times, I am not the expert on your life — you are. As women, we are expected to buy into a whole bag of societal expectations about who we are and how we are. We are often stripped of the dignity of knowing, at a deep level, what is right or wrong for us. The older we are, the more likely this is to be true. We learn early not to question "experts," usually men in positions of authority. Can you recall ever feeling fearful of asking a doctor why he was prescribing a particular medication for you? Or how you might react to that medication? Do you ever find yourself doubting that a doctor's care or repairman's service was truly required? What did you do about it? Many women were taught to accept silently the offerings of those in authority. After all, how could you possibly know more than the "experts"?

For too long women have been told that their problems are all in their imaginations, that there are physical reasons for their emotional problems or vice versa. Each step of the emotional way, women's perceptions are invalidated. Although the situation is changing, we know that when a woman feels depressed around the time of menstruation, it is assumed her emotional behavior is physical in nature: raging hormones. Conversely, if she complains of ailments for which a doctor can find no physical basis, she is told it's all in her head. The medical and psychiatric communities, still dominated by male clinicians, treat women as if they have no ability to assess accurately their own health physical or psychological.

Being told they don't know what they are talking about regarding their own minds and bodies has led to generations of women who don't trust themselves, don't trust other women and don't permit themselves to know their full potential. This is a book about changing that. This book is designed to encourage you to trust your feelings and your instincts. It is intended to offer you a means of assessing your own behaviors and a glimpse into how counterproductive behaviors can be related to unexpressed anger. It's about not finding excuses for why you feel how you feel, but rather giving yourself permission to have those feelings. This book is about *empowering* yourself.

Think about the ideas presented here and see if they don't make sense. You've been told often enough what's wrong and what's right for you. Now you are being challenged to decide for yourself. More than anything, you are being asked to take a chance on you. Go through the exercises in the book as honestly as possible. Open your mind to the possibilities. Talk to people with whom you feel safe. Ask them about their anger and explore your own. Ask yourself tough questions: "What's going on at those times when I feel most depressed and immobilized? Who am I angry with? Why am I angry? What am I afraid will happen if I get in touch with this anger?" I contend that the only thing you have to lose is your depression.

Lois Frankel

1

Anger Turned
Inward

*Behind the depressed woman's anger is an
energetic movement, an impulse that represents the
desire to stop another from causing her pain.*

Janice Wood Wetzel, Ph.D.

Just the word *depression* is enough to strike fear in the
hearts of many women. As a therapist who treats primarily women, I frequently hear comments like, "I feel a little
blue," "I'm somewhat under the weather" or "I just don't
know what's wrong with me, but I can't stop crying." It is
rare that I have a client come into my office who says,
"I'm depressed."

Why such avoidance of a term so precise in describing
a human emotion? Perhaps the answer lies partially in the

fact that depression is so frequently thought of as a woman's issue. We have no problem talking about ulcers, colon cancer, hernias or mid-life crisis — issues and illnesses belonging to a predominantly male domain. On the other hand, society plays down those illnesses, either physical or psychological, which belong to women. Until recently, illnesses such as breast cancer, Premenstrual Syndrome (PMS) and depression have rarely been talked about in nice circles. PMS, for example, was researched and written about over 50 years ago. The research went largely unnoticed in the male dominated health care field until recently, despite the fact that it has far reaching implications for women.

Premenstrual Syndrome (PMS)

I recall presenting a paper on PMS to a graduate psychobiology class consisting of 23 women, one man and a female instructor. I had studiously researched the topic, prepared graphs, charts and handouts. During my research I found myself becoming angry over the fact that this information was so well buried in the literature compared to other frequently discussed health issues. Sexism in the health care field seemed to be one reason why it wasn't better known as a phenomenon affecting hundreds of thousands of women. This perception was validated when the time came for questions and answers. Many of the women had thoughtful questions showing they knew and understood the topic intimately. The instructor had many good points and contributed significantly to the information I had presented. Finally, the one man in the class raised his hand and said that he felt PMS as a health care issue was merely one that people were "bandwagoning" and that the information available on the topic was misrepresented and blown out of proportion. In essence, he claimed that it was a non-issue.

Without the freedom to talk about matters which are important to us and which affect our health, we come to see these issues as taboo, trivial or non-issues as the man in the group claimed. We are forced either to deny their existence or to try to reconcile their presence. As a society, we have opted for the former. Child abuse, alcoholism, drug addiction and concerns of the differently abled are but a few examples of society's denial. Only recently have we become willing to address these matters openly in public. It is sad to think of the millions of people who suffered in silence due to social ignorance.

The slogan used by advocates for increased funding and focus on AIDS is well taken:

SILENCE = DEATH.

The silence surrounding women's health care issues has resulted in both physical and emotional death for many women.

Women And Depression

The fact is that some of the earliest research in depression clearly indicates that across cultures the depressed population is predominately women. A leading authority in the field of depression, Myra Weissman, and her colleagues conducted research that indicates women have a 20 to 26% lifetime risk for depression and a 6% hospitalization rate. This compares with men who have only an 8 to 12% lifetime risk and 3% hospitalization rate. This means that women are twice as likely to experience depression and hospitalization for depression as men.

One reason for the statistical difference is that when women admit their depression, they fall victim to what men see as the "flaw" inherent in femininity. That is, they are then victimized by men's perceptions that women are too emotional or experience mood swings. For men to admit depression is to deny their masculinity. Men are not supposed to be emotional; they're supposed to be strong, not express feelings and be externally unaffected by life events. The stereotypes we have for gender appropriate behavior have ironically deprived both men and women of the kind of help they need. It's easy to see how societal views affect our acknowledgment of and relationship with our own feelings.

Clients are often amazed when I assure them that they're not "crazy" (a word **they** use to describe how they feel), they're depressed. One therapist shared with me the story of a woman who came to her office feeling helpless and in despair over not knowing what was wrong with her. When my friend told her that she was depressed, the client's anxiety over "not knowing" dissipated and her therapy progressed rapidly. Most women have never thought of themselves as depressed in the clinical sense. Quite the opposite, they try to find ways of denying their feelings of depression or sadness, thereby exacerbating the problem. If I had a dollar for every time a client told me, "Everything is really okay. It's just me being overly sensitive," I'd be a rich woman. Look at the contrast with the stereotypical behavior of men who say when they're angry and have strong feelings. It's no wonder that the incidence of depression in women is higher.

It takes energy to deny feelings or keep them hidden. The mind and body have to work overtime to conceal what's really going on and make it appear, at least on a superficial level, that everything's okay. Since one symptom of depression is this loss of energy, there is often a return to the usual energy level when she is able to confront the denied feelings contributing to the depression.

Take a few moments now to complete the questionnaire below. Answer the questions honestly without taking too much time to analyze each item. The questionnaire is designed to determine whether you are currently experiencing the symptoms of depression.

Symptoms Of Depression

Put a check mark next to each of the symptoms you have experienced for a duration of several days or more over the past several weeks.

1. _____ Change in appetite (increase or decrease)
2. _____ Weight loss or weight gain

3. _____ Loss of interest in activities normally enjoyed
4. _____ Feelings of hopelessness or despair, often accomplished by tearfulness
5. _____ Sleep disturbances (sleeping more or less)
6. _____ Loss of energy or general fatigue
7. _____ Feelings of guilt or worthlessness
8. _____ Indecisiveness
9. _____ Inability to concentrate
10. _____ Recurrent thoughts of death or suicide.

No questionnaire can accurately assess whether or not you are, or have been, depressed. This is designed to give you an idea of how and when to determine whether what you are feeling is depression or just the blues. If for any given period of several weeks or more, you check four or more of the symptoms listed, chances are you are experiencing depression. If so, don't be alarmed, depression is the number one emotional problem affecting people living in the U.S. today. If you are not currently experiencing the symptoms of depression, keep the checklist in mind to help you in the future.

What Is Depression?

Janice Wood Wetzel, in her book entitled *Clinical Handbook of Depression*, does an excellent job of documenting the appearance of depression as far back as two thousand years. She notes that even in the Old Testament, King Saul describes what we today would refer to as acts of suicide and symptoms of depression. Throughout recorded history depression, whether called melancholia, hysteria or dementia, has remained a puzzle. Although it continues to be the leading health problem of our time with indications of increasing incidence, there is still much which remains unknown about the nature of depression. Also, there are those who would argue adamantly that much more would be known about depression if it were a predominantly male illness.

I believe that the perception of depression as a "female" problem is changing and will continue to as we see more reports of suicide among teenagers and the elderly. These two population groups experience the world in ways similar to women. That is, teenagers and the elderly are either ready to function more independently or have in the past functioned independently. Both groups, however, experience their power and control as being impeded by others. This creates anger which, when unexpressed or suppressed, contributes to an underlying sense of depression. All three groups, women, teens and the elderly, are controlled by the wishes of others. As an extreme reaction to this anger and frustration, the act of taking one's life may seem the only way out.

Types Of Depression

It is important to point out that there are different types of depression. Not all authorities agree, but it does appear that depression can stem from psychological, physiological or social factors. Most health care providers would argue that all three come into play in determining the basis for a woman's depression. Recently, the concept of chemical depression has come into the public awareness. The discussion has moved from being exclusive to clinical journals to articles in *Time* and *Newsweek* and talk show programs such as Oprah Winfrey, Phil Donahue and 20/20.

Research suggests that an internal chemical imbalance can cause depressive symptoms which can be significantly reduced when treated with prescription drugs. For those people suffering from such chemical depression, **no amount of psychotherapy alone will help.** A qualified psychotherapist will recognize that possibility and, when appropriate, make a referral to a psychiatrist or other physician for a diagnosis.

I encourage anyone who has suffered for a long period of time or to a severe degree from the symptoms described on the questionnaire and who has not found psychotherapy to be effective, to consult with a psychiatrist for a medical evaluation. Also, if you are not currently in psychotherapy or otherwise being treated for depressive symptoms, you should not see this book as the complete solution to your problem. Anyone who, after completing the checklist, believes she is depressed should see a qualified mental health care professional for diagnosis and treatment and to use this book in conjunction with such treatment.

The underlying premise of this book is that for most women social factors affecting women create psychological and physiological responses which contribute to depression. Once again, this is not to say that this is the only origin of depression, but it is the one that will be addressed throughout this work.

Depression is manifested through four key areas: our feelings, our thoughts, our behaviors and our physical functioning. Let's take a look at each of these separately and examine the implications for women.

Feelings

As mentioned earlier, we've all felt a little blue on occasion. Some of us have also felt great despair. These are varying degrees of depression. For some of us, our feelings are easily recognizable, but others take part in a variety of behaviors designed to deny the existence of feelings. On the depression questionnaire, items number 4, "Feelings of hopelessness or despair, often accompanied by tearfulness," and number 7, "Feelings of guilt or worthlessness," refer to feelings. It is important to see denial as a coping mechanism which has enabled women to exist given infrequent opportunities to express their feelings. This particular defense mechanism of coping will be more fully described in subsequent sections of this book.

Keep in mind that depression is a continuum that goes from mild to severe. At times you may experience different points on the scale. While there may be days when it is difficult to get out of bed in the morning and you feel as if you just don't want to face the day, there may be others when it is absolutely impossible to leave your bed or house and you feel as if you just cannot face the day under any circumstances.

There are always plenty of excuses when it comes to acknowledging feelings. The most frequent comments I hear are, "I shouldn't feel this way," "I have no reason to feel this way" or "Things really aren't so bad, I don't know why I feel this way." Sound familiar? If so, I ask you to consider the following affirmations.

[An affirmation is a message that you want to incorporate into your self-talk. Sometimes these messages are to replace other, less positive messages, and other times they are merely reminders of how you want to be or feel.] You may want to post them on your car dashboard, your bathroom mirror, your refrigerator door or inside your desk drawer where only you can see them. Say them out loud as you read them, and add your own to the list.

Affirmations

1. My feelings are my feelings. They belong to me, no one else.
2. I am entitled to my feelings.
3. I do not have to explain my feelings to others.
4. I do not always have to understand my feelings immediately.
5. My feelings are real.
6. My feelings are okay.
7. Just because others do not understand my feelings does not make them any less real.
8. No one has the right to take my feelings away.
9. No one has the right to tell me how I should feel.
10. There are no such things as bad feelings.
11. No one has the right to make me feel a particular way.
12. I have control over how I feel.
13. _____.
14. _____.

It is crucial for your development and your health that you stop denying or ignoring your feelings. Don't be afraid of your feelings. You won't be condemned to suffer them forever if you acknowledge them. On the contrary, once you allow yourself to feel your own feelings, you'll be able to move away from them as you choose. The denial of feelings is the largest obstacle most women must overcome on the road to achieving personal fulfillment.

Thoughts

Our thoughts are affected in a number of ways when we are depressed. Sometimes we can't concentrate, can't remember, have difficulty making decisions or just see the world as being generally bleak. At these times, we think that things will never change — they'll always be bad. This is what makes thoughts of suicide such a serious consideration. When we are experiencing hopelessness we think, "Why go on if things will never change?" On the questionnaire, items 3, "Loss of interest in activities normally enjoyed", 8, "Indecisiveness," 9, "Inability to concentrate," and 10, "Recurrent thoughts of death or suicide," are geared toward thoughts.

It is important to distinguish thoughts which are colored by the depression from thoughts which contribute to the depression. For example, "My life is so bleak it can never change" and "Suicide seems like the only alternative for me," are thoughts colored by depression. It is likely that these thoughts will change once the depression lifts. On the other hand, "My life is so awful," "I am stuck in a marriage in which I feel trapped," "I am married to a man I despise" and "I have parents who constantly disapprove of my decisions and actions," are thoughts contributing to the depression. Once you are empowered to change the situation, you have taken the steps necessary to lift the depression.

It is important to make these distinctions because you must see that you can be in control to take action and eliminate the depression despite the feelings you are experiencing which would indicate the contrary. When we are in the depths of despair (experiencing feelings colored by the depression), it is often difficult to see what is creating the despair (things contributing to the depression which we can control).

I was reminded of the strong impact of culture on thoughts relating to depression during a recent trip to Indonesia to conduct training for employees of a large corporation. During the course of a five-day training program on Interpersonal Skill Development, one woman in the class received feedback which indicated that she was seen as being somewhat reserved and holding back. In all other ways the woman was perceived by her peers to be highly capable and competent. Her English was the best of anyone I had taught during three trips to Indonesia. During the lunch break she asked if I would meet with her privately. I agreed. Within minutes of sitting down, she broke into tears. She said she felt as if she were "going crazy." During this and subsequent conversations with her, I learned that she was in an abusive marriage, which had taken place only because she had been pregnant, a taboo far worse than in the U.S. She asked for help learning how to "live with" the situation.

As I empathized with her, acknowledging that she must be very angry and frustrated, she looked at me in amazement. How could I possibly know that was how she felt? She said she had been trying to hide these feelings for so long because others, including a male Indonesian psychologist, kept telling her how lucky she was be married at all, especially to a man from a good family. For many years she had been holding in her feelings and blaming herself for all that had gone wrong in her marriage. What the class saw was her reserve. All of this woman's energy had to go into holding back a flood of emotions that no one in her culture wanted to acknowledge. It was clear that her situation contributed to the depression and not vice versa.

The importance of differentiating thoughts and feelings is that you *can* do something about your situation. Regardless of how difficult it may seem at the moment, and due to the feeling of fatigue which frequently accompanies depression, it may seem impossible to muster enough energy to make any changes, but the fact is that you *can* get out of your marriage. You *can* deal with your parents. You *can* address your culture. The problem with dealing with thoughts during periods of depression is that there appears to be no "reasoning" with them. There are times it appears that thoughts have a life of their own. There are those people who suggest that once depression has started, it actually does take on a life of its own. That is, from the point of onset until such time as you are feeling like "your old self," you may be largely guided by the momentum of the depression. This concept holds that the chemical changes taking place inside the body during periods of depression take time to run their course. This is one reason why it may be easier to deal with the feelings surrounding the thoughts. For example, if you can get in touch with how angry your husband and your parents make you, then you can change your thoughts surrounding the situation.

Behaviors

Depression is most frequently manifested behaviorally by withdrawing from social situations and from activities usually enjoyed. Behaviors are often interdependent with physical responses to depression, but behavior can be viewed on its own as diminished social, assertive and communication skills. For each of us, our behavioral response is different.

Lisa is an accomplished artist and a graduate of one of the finest art schools in the country, but after three years of trying to make a living at her craft, she decided to take a job in a printing shop. Her job did not come close to utilizing her true abilities.

Lisa entered therapy because she was bored with her life. She had no energy, she was not relating well to her live-in partner and she was doubtful that she would ever be able to return to her one joy: sculpting.

After several sessions it became clear that Lisa came from a family that did not value her artistic abilities. They were hard-working immigrants who had difficulty understanding what she was trying to do with her life. They thought she should simply get a job that paid well and had good benefits. She should participate in her "hobbies" after work or on weekends. In accepting a job at the print shop, Lisa had chosen to live out the life that was prescribed for her by her family. When she came to see me, she was exhibiting symptoms of depression, including withdrawal from those activities and people most important to her because she was living out someone else's script for her life. As we continued to work together, she was able to get in touch with her anger over how neither her partner nor her family was supportive of her efforts to earn a living using her education and talents. In many ways they actually sabotaged her efforts by making it more difficult for her than necessary. The partner, for example, would compulsively spend money, thereby sabotaging Lisa's efforts to save enough to quit her job and pursue sculpting. Her family would not give her money left to her by her grandmother which Lisa wanted to use to purchase a home that could also be used as a studio.

The behavior Lisa changed was her interaction with the people in her life. She learned to express her anger and to ask openly for support. She also learned that she could make choices free from the pressure of others. As Lisa experienced and expressed her anger, the depression subsided and she slowly returned to those activities and relationships that previously brought her so much joy.

Here are some behaviors that may be cues for you in assessing your own depression. Remember, add to the list those behaviors that you have identified as being significant cues for yourself.

1. Fear of or discomfort with leaving the house
2. Cessation of physical exercise
3. Loss of interest in sex
4. Fear of people
5. Argumentative with others
6. Dependency upon others to take care of things (or you)
7. Loss of interest in personal hygiene
8. Frequent crying
9. Loss of contact or interest in contact with friends or family
10. Abuse of substances such as alcohol, drugs or food
11. Excessive sleeping or loss of sleep (insomnia).

12. Other: _____.

Physical

It is in the area of the physical manifestation of depression that the depressive waters get most muddied. Since the body and the mind work so closely together to produce the total human experience, it is sometimes difficult to determine whether a physical symptom is the result of depression or the cause of it. For this reason, I urge you to schedule a thorough physical exam. If there is something physically wrong, it can be treated, and therapy can proceed more effectively. If no physiological basis can be found to contribute to the depression, then therapy can be sought.

It is important to look at the possibility that the physical symptoms may camouflage emotional problems. Women will deny their feelings if they believe they will be unacceptable to others, but a physical symptom — who can deny that? The name for this is *somatizing*. Women put their emotions into a part of their bodies which express these emotional problems by physically malfunctioning.

For example, the weak link for me has always been my lower back. Beginning when I was in college working on my B.A., my back would bother me terribly when I was under intense stress. I know when I begin to get a backache, there is something bothering me that I haven't dealt with. Since I have become aware of this, serious problems with my back have been virtually nonexistent, while before I might have been in bed for several days.

Physical symptoms are not always so clear cut and dramatic. The most frequent physical symptom of depression is lethargy (questionnaire items 5 and 6). This is the general feeling of being constantly tired, even when no physical or mental exertion has taken place. This symptom makes movement of any kind (even to seek a therapist) difficult. There may be hypersomnia (sleeping a lot) or insomnia (sleep disturbance). Likewise, changes in appetite and weight are common physical symptoms of depression (questionnaire items 1 and 2).

I want to repeat the fact that only in the past few years has attention been paid to the idea that depression in some people may be entirely chemically induced. For these people, no amount of psychotherapy, changes in psychosocial factors, exercise or change in diet will prove ultimately effective. The difficulty in identifying these people is that the symptoms are the same as non-chemical depression and the literature in the field is not fully developed. Many of these people go undetected until therapist and client realize nothing else is working.

Women's physical responses to depression vary. A few of the common symptoms are the following:

1. Weakness
2. Fatigue
3. Change in sleep pattern
4. Change in eating pattern
5. Constipation
6. Diarrhea
7. Nausea
8. Backaches
9. Headaches
10. Muscle tension
11. Irritability

12. Other: _____

_____

_____.

Now that you are more familiar with the manifestations of depression, let's get down to the real purpose of this book. From this point forward we will do the following:

1. Look at how you have been socialized to substitute depression as a means of hiding your real feelings.

2. Examine ways of regaining control of your feelings and your life.

We will explore how finding your anger can help you lose your depression. First, let's examine the relationship between the two.

Linking Anger And Depression

Depressed women often make the claim that they feel powerless and out of control of their lives. A woman might say that what she does or wants makes no difference anyway and that she is somehow merely a pawn in a system that is not designed to reward her. The depressed woman retreats to a place that is safe — inside herself. She is then filled with a brewing storm of emotions, none of which she can put a name to. As a woman at one of my workshops put it, "I feel at times that I will just *implode*."

Many women simply cannot distinguish between anger and other feelings because they've never been permitted to express their anger. Anger has been assimilated into other more socially acceptable emotions. While men are permitted to act out their anger, expressing it openly either verbally or through actions such as fighting, contact sports or shouting, women are cued to act them "in," by participating in behaviors such as eating, sleeping or being depressed. Those who act feelings "in" appear, on the surface, to have nothing wrong. No wonder that the woman in my workshop described feeling as if she would explode inward.

As my private practice of psychotherapy began to grow, I became aware that many of my clients were talented, attractive, competent, bright . . . and depressed. The Austrian psychiatrist, Viktor Frankl, describes this as the *existential vacuum*. That is, in the midst of the appearance of success a person is inwardly filled with despair. A common thread that emerged was that in order to be successful, these women felt they had to be free from feelings and emotions. The weapon that men often use against women in the workplace is labeling them as too emotional, and women accept it. Since emotions are socially unacceptable for men, women operating in a male environment deny their emotions, particularly anger, in an effort to ward off the labels.

It was also evident as these women told their stories that negative feelings of any kind were taboo. I would hear comments like, "I feel like I'm just complaining," "I really have no right to feel this way" or "Maybe none of this is real. I'm just imagining it." The concept of anger was totally foreign. As they related incidents in which anger would be totally appropriate, there was no acknowledgment or sign of anger. There was a denial of anger. This was when the link between anger and depression became so clear. When I would say, "Gee, I think I'd be pretty angry if that happened to me," the response I would often get was something like, "I don't feel angry, just sad." Anger and sadness became interchangeable terms.

How the women in my practice told their stories is equally important. The way in which they shared the contents of the stories was strangely incongruent with the messages themselves. For instance, when telling about abusive parents who denied them their childhoods, these women were often emotionless and even at times lighthearted. Nowhere in the recounting did they have a sense of the terrible loss they had experienced. Nowhere did they express anger at what was denied them. Instead, they had learned to accept their pasts as burdens to be borne without expression of feeling or emotion. The depression these women experienced held the anger in check. The depression became a repository for unexpressed emotions which was very intense, yet inappropriate for display. Worst of all, the depression was socially acceptable whereas the negative feelings were not.

In short, anger turned inward, a frequently feminine phenomenon, creates depression. Each time we deny our feelings, blame ourselves or make excuses for the inappropriate behaviors of others, we turn our anger on ourselves.

It should be clear by now that women are masters at using denial as a means of coping with feelings they believe should remain unexpressed. Having learned early the ramifications of expressing negative feelings, women develop an intricate web of mechanisms for denial.

2
The Denial
Of Anger

*The good, capable, conscientious woman
is more likely to be depressed than
her counterpart.*

Anna Freud

Anita left a message on my office answering machine asking me to call her at her office. After I identified myself, there was a long pause and I could tell that she was trying to gain her composure. Somewhat tearfully, she finally said she had called because she felt as if she was "going crazy and needed help." She was married, with a three-year-old child and a promising career in the advertising field. She had the ability to "have it all" but realized that as a woman there was a high price to be paid for this.

She was in despair over what to do. She was getting tired of "juggling" and some of the balls were beginning to fall.

It is through Anita's story that we see depression as a socially acceptable means that women use to cope with their anger. She came to my office displaying common symptoms of depression: tearfulness, weight loss, decrease of interest in normal activities and the desire to isolate herself from others. As she told her story, it became clear that she was being punished for being a bright and capable woman. Her traditional Italian family, especially her parents and in-laws, expected her to be a career woman *and* the perfect mother/wife/daughter/daughter-in-law.

Anita's family felt that she worked just for the money, not because she was capable and wanted to use her gifts in a career. The way they saw it was that if something were to suffer, it should be her job — not them. Anita was caught between the proverbial rock and the hard place. She knew that she viewed her career differently than the rest of her family viewed their jobs. That is, she didn't see her work as merely a method of supporting herself and her family, but rather as fulfilling and rewarding in itself. What was important to her was not understood by everyone else, so they made it difficult for her to achieve her goals. Anita's energy went toward supporting the goals of others in her family, instead of toward her own.

What alternative does a conscientious woman have when her emotions are denied? When she is expected to be like her mother and grandmother, where does she put her energies? To be different in this society is to ask for a lifetime of being "road-weary." That is, it seems as if the choice is to succumb to the wishes of others or to live a life of constant battle. For many, the answer lies in depression. While we are not always conscious of it, we are angry over our situations and, feeling there are no alternatives, we become depressed. As the existentialist philosopher Jean Paul Sartre put it, "We come to believe that these chains shall give us wings."

As Anita and I worked together, it became increasingly clear that an overwhelming amount of resentment and anger were beneath the feelings of total inadequacy at not being able to keep it all together. Gradually she came to understand how she was turning her healthy feelings of anger inward instead of expressing her resentment and asking for help. Anita's depression dissipated and she began to deal with others on a more adult level. She learned that she had a right to pursue her goals, and the need that others had to control her came from a childhood scenario of being the youngest (and physically smallest) in a large family who felt they always knew what was best for her. Anita learned that it was difficult to stand up for what she believed, but that each time she did, she felt an increasingly greater sense of freedom and control over her own life. Each time Anita chose to say no to others she was saying yes to herself.

Much like other women, Anita was afraid to be angry. She had received the message as a child that if she exhibited her anger, she would somehow be abandoned: physically, emotionally or both. Herein lies the basis of women's difficulty with their anger. We learn early on that anger is not an acceptable emotion. We are given strong verbal and non-verbal messages that teach us to deny our anger.

In order to get in touch with the ways in which you have denied your anger, take a few minutes to think about the first time you recall being angry. Picture the situation and those involved. Now think about the messages you were given about that anger. Were you told that it was all right to be angry? Or were you, like many women, told explicitly or implicitly to swallow that anger? Take a few minutes now to complete the following checklist.

Early Messages About Anger

Review the following checklist and mark each message that followed your attempts to be angry.

1. _____ I was sent to my room until I cooled off.
2. _____ I was told that nice girls don't get angry.

3. _____ I was ignored.
4. _____ I was punished (physically, verbally or lost some privilege).
5. _____ I was threatened with religious implications (e.g., not going to heaven or God wouldn't like it).
6. _____ I was told to turn the other cheek.
7. _____ I was made fun of, laughed at or my anger became a family joke.
8. _____ I had love and affection withheld from me.
9. _____ I was told my anger wasn't justified.
10. _____ I was told anger wasn't ladylike.
11. _____ I was treated as if I were out of control.
12. _____ I was told that I was weak or somehow less of a person for being angry.
13. _____ I was treated as if I had committed a sin.
14. _____ I was told it was a flaw in my character (e.g. "You're just like your father.")
15. _____ I was told I was ugly or in some other way physically unappealing.

16. _____ _____.

Reviewing the statements listed above, you can see why the anger gets turned inward and women begin punishing themselves for even having angry feelings. They internalize the messages so well, they can no longer even identify when they are angry. One of the most common problems I hear from women is that they aren't aware of their anger until they're so depressed and immobilized that they know something is wrong, but can't figure out what and why.

Somewhere along the line women learn that by turning their rage into depression they will not face the alienation of the group that they depend upon for their survival. In Jean Baker Miller's book, *Toward A New Psychology of Women*, she describes the concept of social domination and subordination. In every culture the dominants (those who have power) circumscribe roles that are appropriate for the subordinates. With regard to men and women in our culture, the dominants, men, have clearly indicated their displeasure over the anger of the subordinates, women. Men have effectively convinced women that anger is inappropriate, and generation after generation this message is passed along.

An example of this is seen in the behaviors exhibited by a couple I was counseling. Jeff was divorced and the father of two children, aged 8 and 11. Sarah, also divorced, was the mother of two children, aged 22 and 24. Jeff and Sarah had been dating for 2½ years, living together for the last year. One day Jeff suggested that he and Sarah live separately for a variety of reasons, including the distance each commuted to work and the issue of Jeff's weekend custody of the children. Sarah agreed, thinking that this way their time together would be quality time and, in that regard, more fulfilling.

Sarah came alone to one session about a month after the move. She sat down and within seconds began sobbing. She just didn't know what to do. She had told Jeff how angry she was with the whole situation, particularly the fact that she felt she was being shuffled aside in favor of his children. Jeff's response had been that he didn't want to spend time with her when she was this upset. Since they had limited time, they should be happy when they were together. This is a perfect example of the messages that women get: anger is unacceptable and won't be tolerated. We either get rejected, as in Sarah's case, or in some way punished.

The messages around anger are strong and difficult to overcome. They are tied to our sense of self and femininity. At first we use denial to protect ourselves from experiencing our anger. When I begin working with a woman, I ask her to get in touch with and express her anger. It is common to hear, "What good will this do?" In other words, it is so fear-provoking to ask a woman to touch on the very emotion she is taught to deny that she must find reasons for not doing so.

Women learn to repress their angry feelings at a very early age. It isn't just men who give messages about the unacceptability of anger, after a while the subordinates take on the characteristics of those who are dominant. That is, women begin talking like and espousing the same opinions as men. Even mothers impart ideas and values to their children which are consistent with stereotyped behaviors for boys and girls. One woman who attended a workshop of mine on anger and depression told the story of her mother teaching her brother how to fight so that he could physically express his anger at schoolyard bullies, but *she* was told to remember, "Sticks and stones may break your bones but words will never hurt you."

Think about ways you were given the message early in life that your anger was not acceptable. Recall as many incidents as possible of times when you expressed your anger. Be as specific as you can. How were you made to feel? Who made you feel that way? Take some time to think about your responses.

Incidents Concerning Anger

Incident	Message/Action Taken	How You Felt
With Mom:		
With Dad:		
With Siblings:		

With Teachers:

_____

_____

_____

With Friends:

_____

_____

_____

With Others:

_____

_____

_____

The process of transforming anger from its natural state to a more convoluted but socially acceptable one is complex. As you identify some of your earliest memories of anger, you may be able to detect a pattern. One thing is certain: if you don't give yourself permission to be angry, that anger will not simply disappear. It has to go somewhere. For each of us it is funnelled into another behavior which has more social acceptability.

Some statistics indicate that 90% of us come from dysfunctional families. Initially, the concept referred to ACoAs, or Adult Children of Alcoholics. More recently it has broadened to include anyone who comes from a family where neglect, abuse, shame, intolerance or unrealistic expectations predominate. An intolerance of the right to be appropriately angry, in effect, creates feelings of shame and guilt. If you get angry feelings, but at the same time get the message that it's not okay to express them, then you're left with the impression that there must be something wrong with you.

Children who come from dysfunctional families quickly · learn to accommodate to the family rules in order to survive. To do otherwise would be to risk abandonment. One way in which women accommodate to the rule, "No anger allowed," is to deny the existence of anger and work very hard to camouflage the feeling. A typical behavior associated with this is to spend a lot of time and energy pleasing others. Let me tell you how one woman did this.

I met Cynthia about a year after she had been housebound with agoraphobia for nearly three years. Technically the term translates into "fear of the marketplace," but in common terms it means fear of going outdoors. Agoraphobia has a significantly higher incidence in women than men. At the age of 40 Cynthia began developing irrational fears often associated with the syndrome. While she had been employed for years as a nurse, she now was fearful of driving, of elevators and of a host of other activities most of us take for granted.

There are differing opinions on the causes of agoraphobia. I believe that when a person's defense mechanisms, those behaviors which enable him or her to remain safe in an unsafe environment, begin to fail, more dramatic defense mechanisms take their place. In Cynthia's case, her original defense mechanisms were to be the dutiful daughter, sister and wife. When her dutiful roles weren't working, other defenses kicked in.

Cynthia never had a bad word to say about anyone. She was perceived by others as a peacemaker. When others began to get hot under the collar, Cynthia would be the one to calm them down.

Cynthia came from a family in the Midwest and was the oldest of three children. Her mother was wheelchair-bound resulting from a childhood disease and had herself grown up in an orphanage. Cynthia's brother had cerebral palsy and lived at home until the age of 28 when he was institutionalized. Her father, nearly 20 years older than her mother, was a good provider for the family but was emotionally absent. Feelings were never something that were discussed in Cynthia's family.

Cynthia was a bright, precocious child (she told me about finding the Russian alphabet in the dictionary, learning it and doing her spelling tests in Russian). As the oldest, she often was (and still is) expected to help do things her mother was unable to do. Cynthia made the beds, ran errands, and did other odd jobs that her mother could not do. In short, there was a lot of responsibility placed on her not normally placed on girls her age.

When things would go wrong or Cynthia was disappointed, her mother would tell her not to complain; there were a lot of people worse off than she was. In reality, this was her mother's mechanism for coping. In order to overcome the many traumas she had had as a child, Cynthia's mother had developed the attitude that she had to be strong, not complain and persevere. She did not allow herself to be a victim, which is great, but she would also not allow herself appropriate feelings about her situation and her life experiences. Neither could she tolerate the expression of those feelings in others.

Although not on a conscious level, Cynthia could look at her mother and see that things could be worse. She could have a physical impairment that limited her. Her mother was so strong and seemingly confident, despite her limitations and upbringing, how could Cynthia complain about anything? So instead of being able to express how she felt, Cynthia learned to swallow normal feelings of anger by being an even "better" girl, achieving more, excelling at sports and being popular among her peers. She was known as someone who was always "up" and loaded with energy.

You may wonder what is wrong with this. Cynthia was acting in a way which benefited her. What's wrong is that when we act to avoid expressing how we really feel, then these actions are merely defense mechanisms. They are not authentic, but rather are in the service of denial. Sooner or later these defense mechanisms become counterproductive, although they served their purpose enabling Cynthia to grow up in a house where authenticity was not encouraged. As an adult, the defense mechanisms were no longer necessary. Cynthia could make different choices, but the defense mechanisms which were once functional now were dysfunctional. Instead of protecting, they prohibited her from living authentically.

We all develop mechanisms as children which help us to survive living in homes where our parents' rules may not be our own. As a result, some people find themselves overeating, others use drugs and others, like Cynthia, develop into "good girls" who do everything that is asked and work very hard to please others. As adults, we don't need these defense mechanisms any more. They have outlived their usefulness and we must find other alternatives for getting our needs met. These alternatives, however, are often alien to us. If as children we learn to please others as a way of surviving, how do we as adults learn to please ourselves? We were never reinforced for doing so.

In Cynthia's case, the defense mechanisms began to fail her. She couldn't possibly do enough, be enough or achieve enough anymore. Unlike children, adults have myriad responsibilities and relationships. Sooner or later Cynthia had to disappoint someone or fail at something. The standards that Cynthia had set for herself, and were reinforced by others, were impossible for anyone to maintain, but she was not conscious of this fact.

Our psyches are crafty in terms of protecting us and helping us to survive. Cynthia simply couldn't go on as she was, and the symptom she developed to help her survive was agoraphobia. By staying inside, developing phobias and anxiety over external things, Cynthia was able to avoid life's many pressures and the continual expectations of others. Again this is not a conscious process, but rather one which takes place in order to help us counteract the now dysfunctional defense mechanisms we learned as children.

Cynthia had to learn to develop a whole new repertoire of skills for survival. She had to learn to slow down, to say no to people, to allow herself to fail and to be able to express her anger and other legitimate feelings. These were things she was not allowed to do as a child but had to learn to do as an adult in order to survive. Cynthia's transformation of anger took place over many years. She continues to struggle to unlearn those behaviors that worked well for so many years, but she is now beginning to understand how to live a full authentic life and remain in control of her choices and decisions.

3

The Transformation Of Anger

*A good anger acted upon is beautiful
as lightning and swift with power.*

Marge Piercy

Where does unexpressed anger go? If we aren't allowed to express it, do we just stop being angry? NO! It is more likely that we learn to turn this anger into other more socially acceptable, but dysfunctional, behaviors.

For example, one client came to me expressing concern that she was gaining weight and sleeping too much. She said she had little energy for the things she usually enjoyed. As we explored critical events over the past few months of her life, it turned out that her supervisor at work had unexpectedly given her what she perceived to be an unfair evaluation. This meant that her raise would be less than she had anticipated and it would be difficult for her to transfer elsewhere in her company.

Toward the end of the first session I commented that I would be pretty angry if I had been unfairly evaluated. She looked at me with genuine surprise and said, "I don't feel any anger, but now that you say that, it rings true that that's what's going on inside." The client had channeled her anger into, what is for women, socially acceptable forms of behavior — eating and sleeping. As it turned out, she rarely expressed anger openly, either at work or home. Our work together focused on finding ways in which she could comfortably express her anger.

Let's take a look at some behaviors that we use as coping mechanisms which enable us to avoid our anger.

Placating

Since the perceived ramifications of expressing anger are so frightening, we've learned to avoid it at any cost. Placating is one way in which we avoid our anger. Women are notoriously good at "smoothing the waters."

I had been working with Barbara for nearly a year. Her office was located only about two blocks from mine. She would start therapy and then claim that something had happened at work which would preclude her coming for several months. After a time she would call and start again. Even though I would point out to her that this behavior was counterproductive and symptomatic of several of her issues, she said she didn't want to make any waves at work. If she was asked at the last minute to stay late, she couldn't conceive of saying no or excusing herself for an hour and coming back.

One day I remarked to Barbara that even though she complained about things never changing, she didn't appear to be too upset by it all. Each week that she attended sessions she recounted with little or no emotion instances when she was taken advantage of and mistreated by others. I commented that the message was somehow incongruent with how it was delivered. Events were taking place which affected her profoundly, and about which she had strong feelings, but she described them in words devoid of emotion. I pointed out that this matter of fact recounting of events, especially combined with her Southern drawl, gave the impression that she was not someone to take seriously. It was difficult to take her seriously if she didn't take herself seriously and I was no different from most people she came into daily contact with.

Barbara went home and really thought about our session. At the next session she reported that she had asked several people if she came across as strong and serious. The feedback she received was that she gave the impression that she was somewhat of a "Southern Belle." Long before the movie *Steel Magnolias* became popular, I learned what the expression meant. For this client vowed to become just that — lovely on the outside but tough on the inside.

Placating takes many forms. Think about what it's like not to be taken seriously and how it ties in with the depression/anger theme. What happens when you are serious about something? What are the messages you are giving? In what ways do you dilute your own sense of power by devaluing your messages? The most obvious way in which women placate, thereby devaluing their power, is through inappropriate smiling. When men want to make a serious point, they don't smile but women do. The receiver of the message is then left feeling confused. Many women fear their own sense of power and, therefore, act in a manner which softens it. They soften their messages for fear of being perceived as "bitchy" or not feminine. They may put a powerful message out, but quickly pull it back by smiling or laughing and then wonder why no one takes them seriously.

I came across this dilemma not too long ago during a workshop I was conducting on supervisory skills. I was discussing the appropriate behavior for conducting a termination interview with an employee who had received sufficient prior counseling and warnings. I had already spent a day and a half with the workshop participants discussing various aspects of supervision and the group had been quite responsive. During this particular exercise I chose a woman from the group to role play the employee being terminated. I carefully explained to her why she was being dismissed, what would happen from the employer's end (e.g., final check and vacation accrual) and gave her the opportunity to express her feelings. Although I listened sympathetically to her pleas to be kept on, I never waivered in my assertion that she had been given many opportunities to correct the problem behavior. I never smiled throughout the exercise, wanting to make it clear that I was serious about the action I was taking, but I did use body language to convey the message that I understood how difficult it was for her.

At the end of the exercise several men commented on how "cold" I had been. They felt that I acted remote and unfeeling. In contrast, the women expressed the wish that they could communicate with such power and directness. The women in the group didn't feel a coldness at all, merely a serious delivery of a serious message. They read my nonverbal cues correctly and could see that I was sympathetic but unrelenting.

Through this experience I came to realize that men indeed have preconceived notions of the behavior they expect from a woman inconsistent with their own behavior. On many occasions, in similar exercises, I have observed men "terminate" employees with identical affect and delivery. Never have I heard them receive feedback suggesting they lacked compassion.

This is the double bind that women are placed in. They can express their anger in a direct but non-placating way and be accused of being cold or "bitchy," or they can placate others, soften their messages and run the risk of not being heard or taken seriously and become depressed.

Passive-Aggressive Behavior

Another behavior that women use to disguise their anger is similar to placating but has another dimension. Instead of simply doing what others expect of me and smoothing the waters, I tell them that I'll do what they want but do what *I* want in the end. This is described as *passive-aggressive* behavior. We act passive-aggressively each time we agree with someone to their face and then sabotage their efforts behind their backs. The dissatisfied restaurant customer who smiles and says everything is fine when asked how the meal is, but leaves no tip is behaving in a stereotypically passive-aggressive fashion.

Women act passive-aggressively when they tell the boss, "Get the report done tonight? Sure, no problem," but are really thinking that it was unreasonable to expect the report to get finished in such a short time. Then they do not do the report at all. The employee gets angry at an unreasonable request, doesn't express the anger, promises the report will be done and then fails to come through. No one would dispute the reason is acceptable, except that it's not the real issue and displays a "back door" approach to meeting one's needs. The action is really a more subtle form of aggressive behavior, but acted out in a passive way.

These passive-aggressive behaviors serve to get us what we want (or avoid what we don't want), but they do so in a manner which tarnishes our integrity. Acting passive-aggressively is a response of fear, not empowerment. I don't feel as if I can say what I really think so I act out what I think. I may meet my goal when I act passive-aggressively, but I've damaged the relationship in the process.

The behavior must also be viewed as a means for women to get their needs met in an environment that does not listen to them or will not hear what they are saying. While passive-aggressive behavior can be thought of as a coping mechanism, it has the detrimental effect of forcing a woman to lie to get what she needs. This will eventually contribute to depression since most women do not really want to get their needs met at the expense of others.

Shutting Down

A common defense mechanism to combat frightening or potentially dangerous situations is simply to shut down emotionally. We see this pattern of behavior in the fight-or-flight response. When confronted with what is perceived to be a potential disaster, we have two options: to fight or to escape.

Early theories about the roots of mental illness hypothesized that exposure to early trauma caused patients to withdraw from their surroundings. Current literature on multiple personality disorder suggests that the development of alternate personalities results from extreme forms of child abuse, including sexual molestation and emotional or physical battering. Unable to cope with threats to its existence, the human psyche retreats. Not surprisingly, women predominate the population of those with multiple personalities.

Similarly, women who are unable to withstand the pressures of a society that wants them to be seen but not heard, simply shut down emotionally. These women can no longer make choices related to what they want and need, but rather go placidly along with what is expected of them. Their anger becomes a non-issue since they don't even feel it.

Pamela, a woman in her mid-40s, sought help because she just didn't know what she wanted to do with her life and her career. When I expressed confusion over why someone with her professional background and obvious intelligence was unable to define what she wanted, she became distraught. Her entire life she felt she had done what others expected of her. She always wanted to be an architect but her father expected her to become a nurse. As a senior in high school Pamela was accepted at some of the finest schools for architecture, but her family would not provide either the financial or moral support necessary for her to attend one of them. Despite this, Pamela worked several jobs and went to a less prestigious school to get the training she needed. She eventually graduated with a degree in architecture, but each time her career faltered, as our careers often do, she heard her father's voice telling her she would never amount to much. It became increasingly difficult for her to work in a field that she enjoyed but over which she felt there was a cloud hanging. Growing up she never received support for her decisions or her dreams.

Soon Pamela simply shut down. She could function well on a daily basis, providing no one criticized or confronted her on work-related issues. She acknowledged that she was technically skillful in her field, but she was a woman simply going through the motions of life.

My work with Pamela focused on early childhood issues. Feelings of regret for a childhood devoid of nurturing and love were apparent, but nowhere was anger present. The anger over the refusal of her parents to provide attention or support her career choice had simply been shut off. She could feel little emotion other than profound sadness and had difficulty trusting her own judgment. This scenario is not uncommon. Women whose past choices have not been validated and encouraged find themselves frequently doubting their abilities and decision-making capabilities.

People shut down in different ways. Some, like Pamela, go through the motions of life, never feeling anything too intensely, while others become more depressed and withdrawn. These are the women who are reconciled to what they perceive to be their lot in life. They see no sense in trying to change things since they believe that they have no control anyway. This concept of *having the ultimate right to control our destiny* is critical for personal growth.

Compulsive Behavior

Normal everyday activities like eating, exercise, work or sex become compulsions when we feel as if we have no control over the behavior. It's as if the activity takes on a life of its own, directing *us* and not vice versa. We frequently hear compulsive eaters say, "I don't know what happened. I just couldn't stop eating." Or we've seen athletes, exhaustion overcoming their senses, continue on in athletic events long beyond the point of physical safety. Anyone watching the 1984 Olympic Marathon will never forget the moment Greta Waite painfully made her way across the finish line. Her physical resources were severely depleted to the point of being life-threatening, but she persevered. Such are compulsive behaviors. They defy rational thinking.

It is somewhat paradoxical that this apparent lack of control is, in reality, an attempt to have control over something in one's life. In the case of eating disorders (e.g., bulimia or anorexia) these women (and most cases of eating disorders do involve women) have been rigidly controlled and given strict messages about appropriate behavior and looks and have assumed control of their lives in the only way they believe possible. Denied the opportunity to say what they really feel and do what they really wish, the women can and do control the ingestion and expulsion of food.

Another aspect of compulsive behavior is avoidance. In the case of workaholics, non-stop activity serves as a means of denying and avoiding feelings. We see workaholics of both genders, although the higher prevalence in males may be attributed to the fact that their work outside of the home is more readily visible. It is consistent with the theory that men act their anger outwardly and women act it inwardly. Hence, the gender differences between compulsive eaters and workaholics. However, when women do become workaholics, their behavior is similar to men's, avoiding painful feelings.

Turning Anger Inward

Where there seems to be no acceptable outlet for angry feelings, another method used to cope is turning the anger on ourselves. We see this clearly in children who pull their hair, bite their nails to the point of being painful and mutter barely audible self-deprecating remarks. This is a last resort for those who can find no other repository for anger.

One woman shared with me a particularly heart-wrenching story about her childhood anger. Grace was brought up in a religious household where not just anger but any unpleasant feelings were considered taboo. Children in her family were taught to be grateful for what they had and not to "whine" over what they lacked. While there was a considerable degree of superficial warmth and nurturing, there was a noticeable absence of emotion. When Grace would become angry, she was ignored. After all, with all that God had provided, how could she possibly have anything to complain about? When she was angry, Grace would go to her room and sit in a darkened closet beating herself with a coat hanger until she could no longer stand the pain. While Grace has not beaten herself physically for a number of years, she still punishes herself verbally when she becomes angry about things she feels she *shouldn't* be angry over.

Depression is the ultimate manifestation of turning anger inward. But the question still remains why depression has such a disproportionately high incidence among women. Some research points to the fact that men are simply not permitted to express sad feelings, so their sadness may be better masked. Other research suggests that men have many more acceptable outlets for their feelings, including physical sports and verbal and physical aggression. I strongly believe that nonchemical depression in women is a function of repressed anger or aggression. The connection is painfully clear to me. Over and over I have seen a woman become transformed emotionally and physically after she got in touch with her anger.

Unexpressed anger is the single most significant block to a woman's empowerment. Until she confronts the anger in a healthy way she will feel stuck, unfulfilled, useless and act as if she has no alternatives. After feeling and expressing her anger in healthy ways, which will be discussed later, a woman becomes more fully human, and in turn powerful. Unfortunately, women seek *permission* to do this. When I tell a woman it's okay to be angry, she responds first with disbelief then with relief. Often it is the first time in her life someone has given her permission to be angry.

The psychologist Alfred Adler spoke of "man's striving for superiority" (let's assume the sexist language is a result of Adler's time). By that he did not mean the need to be in competition with others, but the need to utilize our talents to their fullest potential. In fact, Adler lamented the lot of women in a society that held them back. His observation was that women were denied the opportunity to use their natural abilities and this denial led to neurotic behavior.

How do you turn your anger into something else? Right now I'd like you to think about situations in which you became angry and how that anger was transformed into other behaviors. Notice how that expression was detrimental either to you or others.

Methods For Denying Anger

Check each of the behaviors that you participate in when you find yourself becoming angry.

When I get angry, I:

1. _____ Eat.
2. _____ Sleep.
3. _____ Drink alcohol.
4. _____ Use drugs.
5. _____ Watch television.
6. _____ Read.
7. _____ Cry.
8. _____ Avoid people.
9. _____ Feel guilty.
10. _____ Exercise.
11. _____ Apologize.

12. _____ Do a good deed for someone (other than myself).
13. _____ Kick the dog.
14. _____ Withhold love or affection.
15. _____ Deride myself.
16. _____ Others. Be specific:

_____

_____

Let's face it. As women, we have developed lots of great ways to mask our anger. With the messages we were given when we were young, the internalized self-messages we give ourselves now and our fear of what will happen if we give ourselves permission to be angry, we have built walls so high around our anger that even *we* have difficulty identifying it.

The first step on the road to wellness is identifying and feeling the anger. Easier said than done. We're talking about changing something that is at the very core of who we are. Women are socialized to be people-pleasers, nurturers, accommodators. We are not supposed to be angry. We are supposed to be for others, not for ourselves. How then do we break the cycle of self-deprecation? The next chapter will help you to identify ways of experiencing and expressing your anger.

4

Finding And
Losing Anger

Here is a strange paradox.
Woman instinctively wants to give, yet
resents giving herself in small pieces.
Anne Morrow Lindbergh

One theory in scientific studies suggests that the degree of power experienced by an organism is dependent upon its ability to capture and use the energy around it (Wood Wetzel, 1984). In our culture women are the givers not the receivers of care and nurturing. They are taught to give away this energy for the benefit of others. No wonder women are often left feeling powerless. The energy required to empower themselves is given away to others in bits and pieces for their use. To ask a woman to be in touch with her anger about this situation is to ask her to deny the lessons she has learned since childhood.

Another process is yet at work here. In an earlier chapter I briefly mentioned that for a woman to be angry she must, in some regards bite the hand that feeds her. In a system of dominants and subordinates, as described in Jean Baker Miller's book, *Toward a New Psychology of Women*, a woman comes to believe this is the way the world should work. To give away one's energy does not seem like an unusual or inappropriate behavior. To the contrary, it seems as normal as eating and breathing. Another author, Anne Wilson Schaef, likened the predicament of women in our society to what it's like to live in air pollution. In *Women's Reality*, Schaef makes the claim that if we live, work and play in pollution long enough, we come to believe that this is how air is supposed to be. We believe denying our feelings, particularly anger, is how life is supposed to be. How, then, can we notice when the air is polluted? Or when we are angry?

When Are You Angry?

It is imperative that women take the time to get to know their "red flags." For all of us, there is a moment when the anger surfaces and in a fraction of a second is swallowed and turned into a socially acceptable emotion or behavior. What are *your* red flags? They're different for each of us. What pushes my buttons may not necessarily push yours. When you are taken advantage of, spoken down to or mistreated in some other way, a logical response should be anger, not depression. Unfortunately it *is* often depression.

The best way to help you get in touch with your angry feelings, particularly if they're frightening for you, is to approach them in a safe way. If I were to ask you to be angry with your mother for ignoring your needs for love as a child or to be angry with your boss for always giving you the assignments no one else wants, it might be difficult. I'd probably be asking you to do something that does not come naturally. Instead, I invite you to follow me on a journey in your mind. This is to be a safe caring trip that will proceed only as fast as you want it to. In this exercise I first ask you to visualize yourself as powerful and in control and next confront someone with whom you are angry.

In order to prepare for our journey, which will take about one hour, you should go to a place where you feel safe and comfortable. You may want to lie down on the floor or sit in an overstuffed chair with your feet propped up. Anywhere that you are physically comfortable and emotionally safe is a good choice. You may want to have a friend help you with this by reading the instructions slowly in a soft, gentle voice. Another alternative is for you to read the instructions softly into a tape recorder. You may want soothing music (with no words) playing quietly in the background. If neither of these alternatives feels right to you, then simply read the instructions several times, until you feel comfortable repeating them silently to yourself with your eyes closed. You need not remember everything perfectly. Simply focus on the essence of what is written and, most importantly, give yourself permission to feel whatever emotions surface.

This exercise will enable you to relax and concentrate on the feelings we are about to explore. Remember, you are in control at all times. You can stop this exercise whenever you wish. I merely ask that you give it your best shot and not go with the easy way out: stopping in order to avoid an uncomfortable situation. New situations are often uncomfortable, but it is these same situations through which we often grow. As the saying goes, "No pain, no gain."

Relaxation Exercise

You are in a meadow where there are lovely flowers, birds singing and a gentle warm breeze blowing. All around you there are sloping hills covered by lush green grass and you feel enveloped by a sense of calm and serenity. As you envision the scene and feel the warmth of the sun on your face, concentrate on the rhythm of your breathing. Take deep breaths and exhale slowly. As you slowly breathe in and out, in and out, allow yourself to be aware of any noises around you but also tell yourself that they will not disturb you as you go through this experience. As you concentrate on your breathing, feel yourself begin to relax. Give yourself permission for this experience to be the only thing on which you currently concentrate. Look around the meadow and experience its beauty and serenity. Feel yourself relax more and more with each breath in and out and in and out.

You see no one and feel quite safe in this meadow. You are alone with your thoughts and feelings. Continue breathing slowly in and out and in and out for several minutes until you feel completely relaxed and at peace. Feel the tension of the day slowly drain from your limbs. You can almost see the negative energy flowing smoothly from the tips of your toes and fingers and evaporating into the air around you. You feel calm and relaxed. With each breath you drift deeper and deeper into a peaceful, but aware state of being. Continue breathing in and out, in and out until you are relaxed and ready to continue on the journey. Take at least ten minutes for this portion of the exercise.

Once you feel completely relaxed and at peace, picture yourself walking around in this meadow. Explore the trees and flowers. Feel the clean air filling you with peace, contentment and energy. You want to experience your surroundings. You are not afraid. You are safe and aware. You begin walking up a gently sloping hill. As you walk you notice different kinds of flowers, rocks and birds. Every so often you stop, look around, then continue up the hill. All around you is blue sky and nature. You can walk as long as you like and you will not feel tired. To the contrary, you will feel more and more energized and excited as you continue on the path up the hill.

You notice a cave in the side of the hill and decide to explore it. It is a safe cave. There are no animals inside it. You are certain of this. You peek your head in the cave, and you are amazed at its beauty. There are glimmering lights and mirrors which reflect each other and you.

The cave is a comfortable temperature. You walk in further and continue to bask in the glow of the lights and reflections. You feel safe and in awe of what you see. Take a few minutes to walk around the cave and experience its wonder.

You suddenly catch a glimpse of yourself in one of the reflections. You are pleased with what you see. You see yourself as confident and self-assured. You may be surprised at how powerful you look. Continue looking at yourself and examine what it is that makes you so powerful and confident. Is it how you are standing? What you're wearing? Notice your eyes, your nose, your mouth and your chin. They all exude control and self-confidence. At first you may want to look away, but your eyes always return to see what a self-confident and assured *you* looks like.

Next, experience what it feels like to be confident, self-assured and in control. You are relaxed. You feel confidence and assuredness running through your body creating warmth and sense of security. You feel powerful and in control. You are safe. Get in touch with what being in control means to you. Continue to look at your reflection in the shimmering glass and say to yourself, "I am confident, calm and in control." Say the message as many times as necessary until you begin *feeling* confident, calm and in control. If something you are experiencing brings you tension or discomfort, return to your deep breathing and avoid the inclination to open your eyes and stop the experience unless it is absolutely necessary. Remember, you are in control. You have nothing to fear.

When you are ready, envision a person who makes you feel angry. It may be someone from work, home or someone with whom you have only sporadic contact. Picture this person as vividly as possible. Look at what they're wearing, the expression on their face and how they are standing. Give yourself a moment to fully experience the person. You don't have to do anything now. Remember that you are calm, confident and in control.

As you feel what it is like to be in the room with this person, be aware of what your body is doing. Is it getting warm? Are you perspiring? Is your heart beating fast? Is your breathing fast or slow? Listen to your body. Ask it to tell you what it is saying. What is the message your body is trying to give to you? Listen to your body for a moment.

Next, ask yourself what are you feeling? Are you fearful? If so, what are you afraid will happen? Are you agitated? Again, ask yourself the question, "How does this person or situation make me feel?" For as long as possible stay in the situation. Avoid the temptation to leave. Experience as fully as possible what it feels like to be present with someone who makes you angry.

Now picture yourself speaking. You are talking directly to the person. Speak freely (either to yourself or aloud) and without fear of retaliation. If necessary, stop and give yourself permission. Repeat, "I have the right to express my feelings" as many times as necessary. If you become frightened, repeat, "I am calm, confident and in control." Focus on the words that you use with this person. You have a message to give to him or her. Picture yourself giving this message in a direct, confident, and secure manner. What is it that you so desperately want to say? Don't censor or block the words. Remember, you are safe and have the right to express your feelings.

Ask yourself the question, "What about this person makes me angry?" Fill in the statement, "I am angry because . . ." Give yourself permission to be angry and feel the full extent of your anger. You may be rageful, you may be tearful or you may picture yourself being physically violent. Whatever the manifestation of your anger, it's okay. Continue to give yourself permission to experience the anger, whatever its form.

Stay in the cave with this person for as long as is necessary for you to be completely heard. If you feel that you are not being heard, say that. Don't allow yourself to be ignored. Picture yourself strong, powerful and straightforward. Let there be silences when you are gathering your thoughts for what you would like to say next. Picture the person standing (or sitting) there waiting for you to finish.

Once you feel that you have addressed your anger, remain in the cave with the person long enough to compose yourself. Picture yourself feeling content with having expressed your feelings. Experience the calm of being heard. Tell yourself that there will be no negative repercussions which you are not capable of handling. Feel the strength that you have acquired through self-expression. Breathe deeply and with each breath feel a sense of power and control over your life. Tell yourself, "I am in control of my life. I make good choices for myself. I have the right to be heard."

Now, say goodbye to the person. Picture this person leaving and as they do, you know there are no hard feelings. As the person leaves the cave, you are feeling calm and in control. Tell yourself, "I can be angry and it will not mean the end of the world. Expressing my anger is healthy."

Stay in the cave a few moments longer and look around at the reflection of yourself in the shimmering glass. You are pleased with what you see. You appear calm, confident and in control. You are proud of yourself for having expressed your anger. Feel the pleasure that comes from taking control of your life. Stay in the cave until you are ready to leave.

When you are ready, picture yourself walking out of the cave. You are walking away from the cave and back down the hill. It is still warm outside. You now feel more powerful than you did when you went up the hill. As you continue walking, feel the sense of calm, confidence and control throughout your body. When you see the spot in the meadow from which you began this journey, walk toward it. Find a comfortable place to sit down. When you are ready to leave the meadow and complete this journey, begin counting backward from twenty to one. With each number feel yourself returning to full awareness. Energy is coming back into your limbs. When you reach the number one, you will open your eyes and be fully awake, alert and refreshed. You will continue to feel peaceful, calm and in control of your life. Once your eyes are open, rest for a few moments and reflect on the experience.

It may be necessary to repeat this sequence several times before you become comfortable with the exercise. Once you are, though, it is a wonderful way of getting in touch with your innermost feelings and fears. While we are applying the technique to anger, you can do essentially the same thing to get in touch with other emotions which may seem elusive to you. The idea is to relax and give yourself permission to experience your feelings.

When you are ready, respond to each of the following questions to understand more fully your reaction to the last exercise:

1. When I first began relaxing, I felt _____

_____.

2. I initially had difficulty relaxing because _____

_____.

3. I chose that particular person because _____

_____.

4. This person reminds me of other situations in my life in that_____

_____.

5. When I first thought about being angry, I _____

_____.

6. The messages I gave myself in order to stay focused on the person were _____

_____.

7. As I expressed my anger, I felt _____

_____.

8. I came to realize my greatest fear around my anger is that _____

_____.

9. When I envisioned myself walking away, I felt _____

_____.

10. The main thing I would like to remember from this exercise is that _____

_____.

5

Fear Of Power
And Control

The paradox of control is that the more
you give away, the more you have.

Barbara Stephens, Ph.D.

Most of the women I see in my practice have a difficult
time with the concept of letting go of the little power and
control that they have. The concept of letting go of control
in order to gain more control seems oddly incongruous at
first. Once you have experienced it, however, you will
know what it means to be truly in control.

The concept that giving up control is empowering played
itself out in our household when we recently returned
from vacation. While we were gone, we had a friend stay

in the house, mainly to take care of Buffer, our dog. The day of our return we were watering the back yard and a neighbor (whom we see only once or twice a year) came storming out. It seemed that Buffer had been outside every night, whining loudly for hours. The neighbor went on at length about how her sleep had been disturbed and how she would take more drastic steps if this ever happened again.

Not the most patient person in the world, my partner wanted to lash back at the neighbor. The thoughts, "Who is she to say she'll take more drastic steps? It's a good thing she didn't because I put up with lots from her household," were all kept in check as the neighbor went on and on. When she finally finished, my partner said, "I can see how you'd be really upset. I would be too if I lost all that sleep. I'm really sorry for this. We thought we had the bases covered by having a friend stay in the house. I promise you we'll take every precaution to see that this doesn't happen again." With that the neighbor acquiesced and said she understood, that the dog was so good normally she knew something had to be different these past few weeks. Rather than having begun a war which we would have to live with or move away from, my partner came in the house feeling very empowered by having given up so much control.

Let's go back to Anita for a moment as another example of the illusion of control. Remember she felt everyone else had more control over her life than she did. In fact, it was true that she gave everyone else's opinion a lot more credence than she did her own. The reason she began seeing me was because she no longer trusted her own judgment. She was an incredibly bright woman who had come to doubt her ability as a wife, mother and employee.

Anita's method for coping in this situation was to be on top of everything going on around her. At work she found herself resentful of the fact that she was one of the few people who was willing to work overtime to get jobs done.

At home, she cleaned compulsively. I couldn't help but show my amazement when she told me she hadn't cleaned behind the refrigerator *this month* and was terribly upset over being such a poor housekeeper. During her sessions she would often defer to me as an expert on child behavior (despite the fact that I told her I had no special expertise in this area nor did I have any children of my own) in an effort to decide whether something she did for her child was acceptable.

In short, Anita felt so out of control of her life that she needed to maintain control in every other way she possibly could. Her compulsions around cleaning and work spoke to this fact. She was driving herself crazy trying to maintain some semblance of control by striving for perfection in everything. Anita had to learn the difficult lesson that it is impossible to maintain this degree of control because in reality we have no control over the actions and opinions of others. *The only thing we are truly in control of is ourselves,* particularly our response to what happens to us. We are not in control of the event itself and it is illusory to think otherwise.

Ironically, this is precisely the kind of control women tend to give away. Feeling that we're not heard, we resort to swallowing our opinions and needs and allow others to decide for us. Certainly at times others do decide for us but we are still in control of our response to the decision. I would have to agree with clients who say, "I had no control over the fact that I was born into an abusive family." My response to this is "But you *now* have control over how you respond to what life has handed you."

Recall the case of Jeff and Sarah. Sarah realized she had no control over Jeff's response to her dilemma, but she did have control over her own response to Jeff. While at first she wanted Jeff to be different and felt she had no recourse, she gradually came to see that she was entitled to her feelings. If Jeff refused to deal with them, even after she explained her needs, then she would be forced to make alternative decisions about this relationship, what it could provide, what it couldn't and what she had to find elsewhere if she chose to stay with Jeff.

The fact is, women are very often angry over feeling out of control of their lives but it is expressed in the form of depression. Each time a woman denies herself her own dreams, wishes and fantasies in lieu of meeting the needs of someone else, she is one step closer to depression. Women are socialized to be for others not for themselves. This socialization is so strong and holds so fast that most women are reluctant to see life any other way. It's the same as the air pollution that Anne Wilson Schaef talks about. We come to believe that this is just the way air is.

When I begin talking to people about getting their needs met, they typically respond that it makes them feel selfish. Or that others might perceive them as being egotistical and self-centered. This fear of what others will think pervades the issue of power for many women. This fear, however irrational, is powerful enough to keep women locked into their depression.

The irony in all of this is that women are very powerful all of the time. They merely wield this power less straight-forwardly than men. Women have learned to compensate for not being heard if they appear to be taking too much power away from men, so they are more covert (manipu-lative) than men. This is particularly true for women who grew up in the early part of this century. The only way they could get their needs met was through manipulation. They were actually very clever at getting what they want-ed, albeit in a circuitous manner. This, however hidden, can still be viewed as a form of power.

During our Leadership Skills for Women workshops, one program describes how to influence others assertive-ly. Nearly every time, there is a woman who raises her hand and says that she can't possibly behave assertively because she doesn't want men to think she's a "pushy broad," a "bitch" or other put-downs men use for women who ask for what is rightfully theirs. What must be understood is that the put-downs are designed to keep us in our place. We have all overheard men making disparaging remarks about assertive women and we fear hearing our name mentioned. So what do we do? We do what is expected of us. We keep our mouths shut. And the remarks have the effect that they are supposed to: They keep us in our places with smiles on our faces.

I am particularly concerned with the incidence of depression in women from age 40 to 60. These are women caught in the middle between the generation of women who knew their roles as subservient help-meets and the generation of those active in the women's liberation movement (or at least beneficiaries of it). They have some consciousness about what it means to have rights, but they also embrace the traditional values they were taught. They know something is wrong but can't quite locate it. They know life could be much more fulfilling but are surrounded by women in their age group who keep quiet about how they can achieve happiness. They all grin and bear their lot in life.

Since my father died in 1985, my mother has been struggling with this issue of getting her needs met. Although a staunchly independent woman her entire life, she has still been one who "knows her place" in terms of male and female social roles for women in her age bracket. When my father died, she could no longer deny herself by saying someone wouldn't like it if she did this or bought that. In the past, it had been safe to ignore her needs because she could always say my father didn't approve or wouldn't let her. Suddenly things were different. On her own for the first time in her life, she continued to behave as if someone were still telling her what to do. In fact, she transferred many of these messages to others, mostly male, in the world at large. Now she was afraid to upset the men in the condominium, my brothers, my uncle or those with whom she worked. For a woman who lived her entire life for others as a nurse, wife and mother, she now had to face herself.

Having read this far, you can probably imagine what happened next. My mother began to call me each week with symptoms of depression. She was tearful, lacked her normal energy level and enthusiasm, experienced a change in sleep patterns and complained of more physical ailments than ever before. During each conversation I pointed out that she sounded like a woman who had no rights. Everyone around her seemed to have more rights. I asked why she wouldn't speak up for herself, at work or with friends and family. The response was always the same: "I don't want to look selfish, as if only I matter." In reality, her behavior said loudly and clearly that she didn't matter at all, which was why everyone else's needs but hers were being met.

Gradually she began asserting herself more. She began to put out more of what she wanted in a straightforward unapologetic way. The depression slowly faded and Mom became more happy and content with her life. She is, after 65 years, learning that this is *her* life. Only she can live it and if she doesn't live it as she wants, especially at this point, then she has made a choice for others to have more control of her life than she has herself.

One of the difficulties with women learning to take control is that it may involve taking something from someone else. Each time a woman asserts herself, she is forced to say to the men in her life, husband, son, father, uncle or male employer: "I want something from you. I want what is rightfully mine. I want my needs met too." With each assertion, this is the message. It can't simply be viewed as telling the boss we need more money, but it gives an implicit message that says, "I'm worth more than this." It isn't just telling your husband you need more help around the house since you work full-time too, but it's saying, "My time is as valuable as yours and I want you to give up some of your leisure time just as I do." It's more than telling your 23-year-old daughter that you will not give her any more money; the real message is, "I'm tired of being here just for *you*. I would like to spend some of the money you want on *me*."

These implicit messages given to others when we take back control of our lives is what makes asserting ourselves so difficult. More than just getting what we want, need and deserve, we are forcing others to give back what we have been giving away to them for so long. The reactions that we get when we try to do this are often difficult to cope with. Remember, others often don't want to change or see the need for change. They already have everything that they want — why give anything up?

Several weeks ago I had dinner with a couple, friends I had not seen for several years. During the course of the dinner conversation, I asked how each of their children was doing. They exchanged looks, sighed and looked down. "Well," began the wife, "our daughter is doing just great. Our son is another story." In exploring this further with them, I learned that their 22-year-old son was not working, was living at home with his pregnant 17-year-old girlfriend and was making no moves to do anything to change this situation. They felt dismayed over their inability to get him to look for work so that he could move out and function more independently.

I said it seemed to me that they really had no control over whether their son got a job or not. That had to be his decision. But I asked them what they really wanted for themselves. They could easily explain that what they really wanted was their household back to "normal." This included their son and his girlfriend moving out as soon as possible. When I asked why this wasn't happening, I heard what normally is said in conversations such as these: "We would feel as if were being so selfish." It was clear to me that they had made it easy for the son and girlfriend to live just the life they wanted at Mom's and Dad's expense. I suggested they were doing their son no favor by allowing him to live in a comfortable environment, and thereby colluding with him to remain unemployed. They had no control over what their son did, but they did have control over their own home.

The next month my friend called to report that she and her husband had told their son he must move out. They said they would be happy to get him started in his first apartment, but after that he would be on his own. The couple reports that this is the happiest and calmest the household has been in years and that their son found a job within a week of moving out.

Resistance to change is normal. However, the response of others has less to do with the validity of your request than with their effort to maintain the status quo. This is the point you must keep in mind. You are not crazy, but others would like you to believe that so they can maintain their comfort level (at your expense of course).

What are the ploys others use to get you not to rock the boat? Not coincidentally, they're very similar to the messages you were given as a child about your anger. Review the following checklist and mark each message you are given when you attempt to get your needs met.

Tactics Used By Others To Deny Your Needs

1. _____ Why would you want to do that?
   (Stated with an emphasis on the "why" and a look of disgust on the face.)
2. _____ I really don't think it's possible at this time.
   (Stated with authority and condescension.)
3. _____ Wouldn't you rather . . .?
   (Read: I would rather . . .)
4. _____ You're joking, of course.
   (The person is incredulous at your suggestion.)
5. _____ Why don't you think about it and then come back to discuss it?
   (You caught them by surprise and they want to prepare their rebuttal.)
6. _____ If you really want to, but don't come crying to me when it doesn't work.

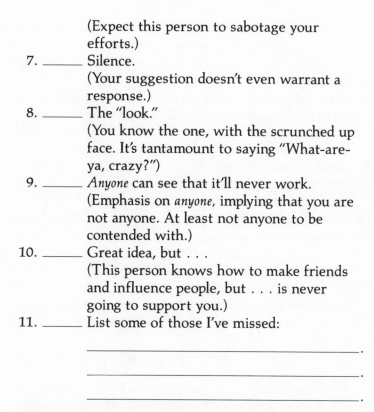

(Expect this person to sabotage your efforts.)

7. _____ Silence.

(Your suggestion doesn't even warrant a response.)

8. _____ The "look."

(You know the one, with the scrunched up face. It's tantamount to saying "What-are-ya, crazy?")

9. _____ *Anyone* can see that it'll never work.

(Emphasis on *anyone*, implying that you are not anyone. At least not anyone to be contended with.)

10. _____ Great idea, but . . .

(This person knows how to make friends and influence people, but . . . is never going to support you.)

11. _____ List some of those I've missed:

_____.

_____.

_____.

All of these tactics are conversation stoppers. They are spoken for the purpose of ending the discussion. When anyone uses any of these tactics, you should know you have threatened the heck out of them. But the discussion doesn't have to end there.

One night a few weeks ago I was talking about this book to my friend Desiree. She really liked the concept but said it was hard to behave differently when she had no model for asserting herself with others. Desiree said that in her family, disagreements were loud, angry and, at times, violent. So she learned to withdraw in the face of disagreement and continues to do that today. She agrees that her bouts with depression often result from unexpressed anger, but she still fears the confrontations that might ensue by her non-compliance.

Desiree is not unlike many women. Who **has** had a model for healthy disagreement and anger? Most of us have rarely **observed** a healthy disagreement, let alone participated in one.

Let's take a second look at the tactics listed and see how you can disagree without withdrawing or losing your femininity. As you go through the list, envision yourself giving each response in a way that is neither angry nor apologetic. Picture yourself looking the person in the eye and be certain to envision a specific person who tends to try to take your power away from you by using one or more of these tactics. Hear the tone of your voice — it is straightforward, relaxed and not too high-pitched. You are not trying to initiate an argument, but state how you feel about the remark or ask for additional information to clarify the speaker's position.

Once you have asked a question, wait for a response. Don't feel as if you have to fill in the silence or explain yourself in great detail.

Tactic	Possible Response
1. Why would you want to do that?	a. Because it's important to me.
	b. Why wouldn't I want to?
	c. I feel as if your question is really a way to put me down. I'd like to discuss it openly.
2. I really don't think it's possible at this time.	a. I don't see why not.
	b. Please explain why.
	c. According to my calculations, I would have to disagree. Let me explain.
3. Wouldn't you rather . . .?	a. No, I wouldn't . . .
	b. I think that's what *you'd* rather. As for me . . .
	c. Perhaps this is a place for us to seek a compromise.

4. You're joking, of course.

    a. No, I'm not. I'm serious.

    b. Why would you think I would joke about something this serious?

    c. You seem uncomfortable about the idea.

5. Why don't you think about it and then come back and discuss it?

    a. I already have given it a lot of thought.

    b. I'm prepared to discuss it now.

    c. You seem to suggest I haven't already thought it through.

6. If you really want to, but don't come crying to me when it doesn't work out.

    a. Yes, I do really want to and I'm not sure it'll work but I'm going to try.

    b. Yes, I do really want to and I'd like to be assured of your support.

    c. Yes, I do really want to, and it may not work out, but then there are never guarantees in something like this.

7. Silence.

    a. Silence (but don't allow the subject to be changed).

    b. I'm not sure what your silence means.

    c. I'd like some feedback.

8. The "look."

    a. I'm not sure what that look means.

    b. I'd like to discuss this seriously.

    c. Am I supposed to take that as a putdown? It feels like one.

9. Anyone can see that it'll never work.

    a. It seems as if you don't think it will. Can you tell me why not?

b. I think it will.

c. I have my doubts too at times but it's something I'm going to make work.

10. Great idea, but . . .
a. I'm glad to hear your concerns. I have my own too.
b. I'm glad you like the idea. How would you overcome the concerns?
c. I'm getting a mixed message from you.

The idea is to take the power back. That is, the power over your life, that you have let others assume for so long, must be in your domain if you are to let go of the anger and depression. Often I hear women say, "I know, I do it to myself." But that's only half of the story. The other half is that there are people who reinforce you for doing it. This is where the collusion is. It's up to you. Taking back the power is not equivalent to having power over anyone. It's about having control of your own life.

Right now think about the ways in which the people in your life keep you in your place. Write down the words, describe the body language and picture the situations that are designed to minimize your power. For each item that you list, get in touch with how the statement or situation makes you feel. Then write down an alternative response that would serve to take back control of your life.

Situation	When It Happens	Alternative Responses

Some other techniques for taking control back include the following:

1. State Your Expectations Clearly. Don't expect that others can read your mind. Be certain you are clear in your own mind what you want and express it.

2. Say No Without Apology. The trap that many women fall into is saying no, then apologizing, feeling guilty and relenting. Once you have determined that no is the only correct response, stick with it.

3. Use "I" Statements. As opposed to "you" messages. Own what it is that you are saying by beginning your sentence with the word "I": I feel . . . I think . . . I would like . . . I wish and I will . . . are all more powerful messages than using phrases like, one would wish . . . don't you feel . . . or everyone believes.

4. Practice "Given That" Messages. As a means of holding your ground while acknowledging someone else's point or rights. For example, "Given that there's a lot of truth to what you're saying, I still think this is the best way to proceed."

5. Fog the Other Person. This is a method of buying yourself time without giving in. Picture a fog going up between you and the person who is confronting you. The fog serves to create a distance and keep you safe. Then use phrases that further keep the purpose at a distance, such as, "I can see this is important to you, can you tell me more?" or "I had no idea this was so upsetting to you. Let me think about it and get back to you."

6

The Illusion Of Inclusion: Women In The Workplace

Great spirits have always encountered violent opposition from mediocre minds.

Albert Einstein

Despite the courses you may have taken in assertiveness and career development, you still have the feeling that there's something you don't know. The books you've read, such as *Games Mother Never Taught You*, *Men and Women of the Corporation*, and *Paths to Power*, somehow don't pinpoint this nagging feeling that something isn't quite right. Belonging to the appropriate formal and informal networks provides only momentary relief from feeling unable to measure up, incapable of reaching the higher rungs on the corporate ladder and plagued by this sense of powerlessness.

Does the above paragraph describe what you feel about being a woman in the world of work? You're in good company and you're right where you've been programmed to be. Playing the corporate game is different for women, as you've read, and does require learning new skills. The books, workshops and networks all provide meaningful pieces of the puzzle.

There's one piece, however, that is often left out and, for many, it's what leads them to the therapist's office or even to abandon their careers altogether. The workplace offers a unique set of challenges for women. Given that the percentage of women in the workplace has dramatically increased over the past two decades and will continue to into the next century, women must come to terms with the factors which negatively affect them in this setting.

Consider the following scenario:

Shirley realizes that the men in her department seem to be getting the prime assignments which provide experiences necessary for upward mobility. She decides to be assertive and discuss this with her supervisor, Pete. She points out, nondefensively, examples of when this has occurred while Pete listens attentively. When Shirley is finished, Pete flatly denies that this is what is happening. He claims it's just "the roll of the dice." When Shirley suggests that he may not be seeing things the way they are, Pete becomes defensive and denies any such thing. He tells Shirley that she is just being "supersensitive." Shirley leaves the meeting feeling frustrated and wondering if her assessment of the situation is correct. The accommodating part of her wants to believe Pete.

In this example there are two important and usually unrecognized systems at work: (1) mystification and (2) domination/subordination. The concepts are closely interwoven, each describing what happens in the workplace and how the status quo is perpetuated. The terms can also apply to any relationship in which one person struggles to maintain power over another.

Recall our earlier discussion of systems. A system, by design, is for the purpose of maintaining the status quo, perpetuating itself and, above all else, continuing in the service of self-preservation. From these workplace systems, women get an amorphous feeling that is difficult to describe, but greatly affects their sense of personal power and control. Professional women often present a dichotomy of knowing on an intellectual level that they are competent but, on an emotional level, feeling powerless and inadequate. As those of you who have experienced it can attest, the emotional feeling is devastating and debilitating. In working with women in such situations, I emphasize the nature of the system which is designed to make them feel this way. Let's take a look at the processes of mystification, domination/subordination and the white male system.

Mystification

Karl Marx used the term "mystification" to describe what happens between members of different social classes, the oppressors and the oppressed. Its application is based primarily on degrees of power or control. Mystification is the process which takes place between people with uneven or unequal amounts of power. The two-part process begins when the oppressed confronts the oppressor with the fact that he or she feels somehow mistreated or abused. The typical response on the part of the oppressor is to deny that any such thing is happening. The second part is when the oppressed person suggests that denial is taking place, underscoring the reality of the situation. In reply the oppressor denies that he or she is denying.

In the brief scenario described above, Shirley confronted Pete with his misuse of power, and he denied there was a problem. When Shirley suggested that he might not be seeing the situation realistically, Pete denied that he was denying. The situation became obscured and the parties perplexed. Both Shirley and Pete were left feeling confused and in some way damaged by the encounter.

Shirley left feeling confused and powerless; Pete feeling defensive over his management decisions.

Mystification is, by design, used to maintain the power structure, not modify it. Shirley hoped to be the recipient of better assignments which would enhance the possibility of upward mobility for her, but that would have altered the power structure which was designed to maintain power in the hands of white males — not share it.

The psychological ramifications of mystification in the workplace are obvious. The feelings of those with lesser power and control are denied and invalidated. They begin to lose their sense of self-confidence and doubt their ability to assess situations accurately. Powerless is the way most people describe the feeling. When this happens, nobody in the workplace wins. Subordinates are unhappy, unwilling to take risks and less productive.

Bear in mind that the underlying dynamic is to maintain the status quo in terms of the balance (or imbalance) of power. If Pete had agreed with Shirley, he would have run the risk of shifting that balance, losing some of his own personal power or that of the other males. The fear associated with this far outweighs the benefits in Pete's mind. This fear of losing power maintains the second system: domination/subordination.

Domination/Subordination

There are two basic types of inequality described by Jean Baker Miller in her book, *Toward A New Psychology of Women*: temporary and permanent. Temporary refers to the kind of inequality that we witness in parent/child, teacher/student or even client/therapist relationships. The person with the power has some "ability or valuable quality" which he or she is supposed to impart to the other. The goal of temporary inequality is eventual termination of the unequal status.

The second kind of inequality, permanent, results from "ascription" or how birth defines one. Race, sex, religion and national origin are all examples of birth ascriptions.

Through this process dominants and subordinates are defined. Miller has suggested that dominant groups "usually define one or more acceptable roles for the subordinate. Acceptable roles typically involve providing services that no dominant group member wants to perform for itself. . . . Subordinates are usually said to be unable to perform preferred roles. Their incapacities are ascribed to innate defects or deficiencies of mind or body."

You've probably already figured out from this description that there are many forms of domination/subordination in our society. Certainly African-Americans in our country have been victimized by this process. People with disabilities also fall into this category as those who are labeled as somehow less than full human beings. The only people seen as being worthy and fully human are the dominants. The legal term placed on this phenomenon in the workplace is discrimination, but in reality we are witnessing simply the process of domination/subordination.

Thus, in such a system women are destined to live their lives being not as good as. Once they realize fully the role that has been ascribed to them, they generally tend to play that role in an appropriate manner. Many women never realize that much emotionally maladaptive behavior results from not realizing they are playing a role. Anna Freud said that it is the good, capable and conscientious woman who is more likely to suffer from depression as a result of her role. At some point, most women accept their lot in life and come to believe in and collude with the system, as if the system knows what is best for them.

The Illusion Of Inclusion

Living in Los Angeles I can appreciate Anne Wilson Schaef's analogy of the white male system to air pollution. Schaef says, "You eat in it, you sleep in it, work in it and sooner or later you start believing that this is the way the air is." For many women, mystification, domination/subordination and the white male system is just the way it is. Our sense of fair play, like Shirley's, denies the possibility that anything specific is excluding us from achieving our potential. In this way we come to collude with a system which gives the illusion that we are included.

Believe it or not, there are rules that govern each of these three processes. The workplace rules are fairly obvious, but seldom verbalized. Even subordinates don't dare to discuss them with each other for fear of being ostracized. The dominants simply deny the existence of rules, which makes it very difficult to take action or effect change. If the myth says there are no rules or processes, then what is there to change or fight? It's easy to see why so many women become frustrated and are rendered powerless by this boxing at shadows. The continuous search for external validation of one's competence inevitably proves fruitless, thus reinforcing the feelings of powerlessness.

Another reinforcing element in the system works in a very powerful way to keep women hooked in. This is a concept of behavior modification called *variable interval reinforcement*. In very simple terms this means that we don't know when the next reinforcing event will happen. Of all the ways that behavior can be reinforced, this is the one from which it is the most difficult to break away. I also call it the *Las Vegas Effect*.

Think about when you play the slot machines in Las Vegas. You put a quarter in and nothing happens. Another quarter, still nothing. After several more quarters, there's a payoff. Normally it's not a lot of money (at least never for me), but enough to keep you hooked. Because of the small amounts of reinforcement you hang in there waiting for *the big payoff*.

In the workplace the same kind of variable reinforcement keeps a woman in a system that will eventually bankrupt her emotionally. Women are given token or minimal increases and promotions. Like the slot machine that pays off minimally, these minor rewards keep us hooked, thinking that the *big payoff* is on its way. So we feed more of ourselves into the system. In reality, few women actually get that big payoff but it's just enough to reinforce our belief that the system works fairly and, with enough hard work (or enough quarters), we can achieve recognition and power.

William Holland, former Manager of Corporate Equal Opportunity Affairs for Atlantic Richfield Company, calls this belief the *illusion of inclusion*. He describes this as the belief of minorities and women that they are included in the upwardly mobile paths. They believe there is room for them in the system in numbers comparable to the room available to white males. The reality is that this is merely an illusion. Despite civil rights laws and regulations, equality in the workplace remains illusory for most of the people these laws are designed to protect. The decision-making power is in the hands of white males who would share it only reluctantly, sparingly and intermittently.

Illuminating Illusion

Women do not need to be bound by these systematic machinations. The first step toward emancipation is recognition of reality. A line from an old textbook has been running through my mind lately: *The essence of normality is the denial of reality.* As long as we deny what is really going on, we serve to keep the waters smooth and "normal." Women must stop colluding with the system, attempting to maintain a semblance of normality and begin to take control of their own lives. If women are to reach their potential, then they must stop living within these proscriptions.

Until we recognize how the system works in subtle ways to maintain the status quo, we cannot work to be free of the constraints. This is no easy task. We are so programmed to accept what dominants tell us that we come to doubt and second guess our own perceptions. In the scenario with Shirley and Pete, this is the trap that Shirley has fallen into. She doubts the validity of her common sense and readily embraces Pete's viewpoint. She has now become an *enabler*, someone who assists in the perpetuation of an unhealthy system.

Can The System Change?

In his book, *The Turning Point*, Fritjov Capra, a physicist, examines where society has been, where it is currently and where it is bound. He sees the world at a turning point. The world's best economists, social scientists, politicians and technical advisors can no longer predict our course. We are at a point where the power structure must change in order to assure our survival as a society.

Capra calls attention to ancient civilizations and asserts that those that survived the longest and experienced continued growth were those in which the dominants had the foresight to relinquish power when they no longer wielded it effectively. Capra refers to the work of the historian Arnold Toynbee, who views flexibility as essential for continued societal growth. Without that, a society is destined to meet its demise: "The dominant social institutions will refuse to hand over their leading roles to these new cultural forces, but they will inevitably go on to decline and disintegrate."

Our present society shows many of the same symptoms that ancient civilizations did as they began to decline. Alienation and increased mental illness, violent crime, social disruption and religious cultism were all present before the turning point. In our society, the dominant social institution for at least 3,000 years has been the patriarchy. A non-patriarchal society is difficult to envision, but Capra claims it is not too far off. He claims patriarchy is no longer working and that the feminist movement is one key factor that will profoundly affect our further evolution.

Women bring a uniqueness to the workplace. We must seek not so much to be like the dominants, but to maintain and integrate our abilities to benefit ourselves as well as the organization. We must regain our individual and collective power through understanding the systems which operate against us. True empowerment comes from knowing there are choices available. We are not relegated to one color, but rather have the full rainbow of colors from which to choose. Each of us must ask how much we are willing to risk and go beyond the assigned role into the realm of the unknown, where we can be recognized as powerful, capable and bright women.

Steps you can take to gain more control of your life will be described in the next chapter. Using all the information previously discussed, try to get in touch with how the system excludes you in your workplace. Then you will understand the system better so you can prepare to counterbalance its effects.

Checklist Of Workplace Excluders

Put a check mark next to the ways in which your workplace system excludes you and merely gives the illusion of inclusion. Then add your own perceptions of how this happens in your unique situation.

_____ 1. You are denied positions or promotions for which you are qualified and lesser qualified men are awarded these same positions.

_____ 2. You are excluded from informal meetings, such as lunch, drinks after work, golf or tennis on Saturday, where business is discussed.

_____ 3. Your ideas are used by others who present them as their own.

_____ 4. You are excluded from formal meetings where decisions are made about the direction of the company or department.

_____ 5. You are not given the assignments which provide a wide range of experience or exposure.

_____ 6. The language in your workplace serves to keep women in ascribed roles (e.g., honey, dear, my girl).

_____ 7. The atmosphere in your workplace serves to keep women in ascribed roles (e.g., sexist jokes or treating women as sexual objects).

_____ 8. The pay structure in your company suggests women are not as deserving as men.

_____ 9. There are female "ghettos" in your company (departments or jobs that are filled predominantly with women and are traditionally low paid).

_____ 10. Women are hired in at a low level of the organization, told that it's a foot in the door but are never given the opportunity to move up (so the system can say, "There's no problem here, we hire women").

_____ 11. Women are given positions with terrific titles and loads of responsibility, but with no accompanying authority nor commensurate pay.

_____ 12. You are told to be patient, your time will come.

_____ 13. _____.

_____ 14. _____.

_____ 15. _____.

7

The Ten Commandments Of Taking Charge Of Your Life

You who must leave everything that you cannot control.
It begins with your body then later turns 'round to your soul.
Well I've been where you're hanging, I think I can see
how you're pinned. When you're not feeling holy,
your loneliness says that you've sinned.

Judy Collins

Taking charge of her life is one of the loneliest things a woman ever does. She is other-oriented. A woman's existence has been predicated on doing and being for others. To suggest otherwise creates a tremendous amount of internal confusion and turmoil. As I begin to explore with women how to make choices which will meet their own needs and wants, nine times out of ten they tell me that would be selfish. Even greater than the concern of feeling selfish is the fear that *others* will perceive them as selfish.

It is often impossible, initially, for them to understand that this is not about living a life that excludes concern for others. I am talking about assuring that women's needs are factored into the equation.

In response to the woman who asks, "If I am not for others, then who am I?" I offer this Jewish saying:

If I am not for myself . . . who will be for me?
If I am only for myself . . . what am I?
If not now . . . when?

By taking charge of her life, a woman is, in essence, saying she is willing to assume responsibility. She is no longer defined by her relationships with others, but rather by her own actions. Although relationships remain important, she can no longer use others as an excuse for staying angry and depressed. By taking charge she admits to having responsibility for others, as does all humankind both on a global and personal level, but she also acknowledges that such responsibility starts with her.

How To Regain Control Of Your Life

I developed the following set of "Ten Commandments" in response to women who wanted to know how to change their lives *right now*. They were tired of hearing that women's equality should be achieved by working within the system. They wanted to know what to do today that would help them function with more integrity and less despair. The Commandments are an answer to the question, "How do I regain control of my life?" After all, what are your options?

1. *You can remove yourself from the system* without attempting to change it or yourself within it. There are certainly examples of women separatists who live in women-only compounds, grow their own food and have their own systems of economics. This is one way to cope with a system that you feel is unhealthy for you.

2. *You can remain within the system* and do nothing differently. The likely outcome of this alternative is that you will continue to feel unfulfilled, resentful and depressed.

Yet it is an alternative and one that thousands of women choose every day.

3. *You can actively work to change the system.* You can participate on committees in support of a woman's right to choose abortion, the Equal Rights Amendment or legislation for child and family care leave. The idea that we must actively work to change the views and actions of others in order to change the system is appealing to some and overwhelming to others.

4. *You can act to take charge of your own life and give up the illusion that you can possibly control the system.* This course of action is often overlooked as a legitimate method of creating change. This provides the least threatening means of defining individual power and control, but it is still potentially threatening. Whenever we make changes in our behavior that are difficult, they can be threatening to ourselves and those who held past control over us. As we take control of our own lives, we are changing the status quo. In order for us to have more control, someone else has to have less. This is why women are often met with subtle and blatant opposition as they make changes in their lives. While blatant opposition is more obvious, such as forbidding some action, the subtler forms of opposition are often more perplexing. For example, a woman with small children decides to go back to school to learn new skills or improve her career opportunities. While her husband may verbally express approval, she may find that he begins to work later, leaving her with no one to care for the children on class nights. She misses classes and then drops out of school. On the surface her husband's working late may appear to be circumstantial, but more likely it is a subtle way of opposing any change in the status quo.

The Ten Commandments Of
Taking Charge Of Your Life

The Ten Commandments of Taking Charge of Your Life provide guidelines for working within the system without losing your integrity and without trampling on the rights of other people.

Commandment One

1. Thou Shalt Give Yourself Permission to Take Charge of Your Life.

It seems like a simple idea, but surprisingly few women do it. Self-talk encourages you to go ahead, make that change from giving away control to being in control of your life; this is not just important, but crucial. If the messages you have received all your life instructed you to put others first, then your task is to reprogram yourself.

By giving yourself permission to take charge of your life, you are acknowledging the fact that you are as important as other people. You are validating the fact that you don't need to be in control of everything and everyone, but merely in control of yourself. You are freeing yourself from the invisible ties that keep you depressed. In short, you are saying, "I am the master of my fate and the captain of my ship. I am capable of taking good care of myself. I know what is best for me."

Commandment Two

2. Thou Shalt Stop Asking Questions and Start Making Statements.

As mentioned earlier, women have always wielded large amounts of control, but covertly for fear of letting others (and themselves) in on how powerful they are. They have had to couch their ideas as questions, rather than affirmative statements. In the office, for example, the secretary might say to her boss, "Don't you think we should begin working on the XYZ report?" The real message behind the question is, "Let's get moving on the XYZ report. It's due shortly and I'm trying to save your hide."

By asking questions women have remained safe. They have not had to assume responsibility for decision-making. They have also given away their control and power. When a woman asks this kind of a question, one of three things happens:

1. She is told no.

2. She gives away her ideas and others assume ownership.

3. She learns that she can only be productive through others (by manipulating them to do what she wants).

To take control back, women must begin to assume responsibility for their own ideas and needs. Again, we can never control others' responses, but we can stop making it easy for them to deny us our feelings and desires.

EXERCISE:

Say the following pairs of questions and statements out loud. Think about how you feel after each one.

Q: Do you think we should paint the house this summer?

S: I think we should paint the house this summer.

Q: Would you like to go to that new restaurant tonight?

S: I'd like to try that new restaurant tonight.

Q: Don't you think it would be better if we used this time to follow-up on the Jones' account?

S: I think this time might best be spent following-up on the Jones' account.

Q: Are you planning to replace that leaky valve this weekend?

S: I'd appreciate it if you would replace that leaky valve this weekend.

One is so much more powerful than the other. When asking a question, we let others decide for us. When making a statement, we assume ownership for what we want and give others the opportunity to do the same. Remember, the purpose of a question should be to gain information that you do not already have.

Commandment Three

3. *Thou Shalt Not Apologize.*

In a workshop recently a woman asked me if it was ever appropriate to apologize. Certainly! But make sure you apologize for your own errors. Too often we apologize for the mistakes of others. Often women say, "I'm sorry, I didn't know that's how you wanted it done." The mistake was made because someone else didn't give adequate information or training. Stop apologizing for the errors and omissions of others.

You may be thinking, "But it's such a small thing. What does it hurt to apologize?" The answer: a lot. Each time we apologize for something we didn't do, we reinforce the idea that we are wrong. We don't really know what's right after all, we're no good and we're stupid. By refusing to assume responsibility for other people's mistakes, we not only cause them to assume responsibility for themselves, but we take back control of our lives. We move out of the victim role and into the role of responsible adult.

Commandment Four

4. *Thou Shalt Make Choices Without Fear Of Making Mistakes.*

One of the lasting things I learned in graduate school is the statement, "We make choices for the best of all possible reasons." No one ever sets out intentionally to make a mistake, but we all make them. At any given moment, we are doing the best we can with the information at hand.

The fear of making a mistake keeps many women paralyzed their entire lives. The irony is that mistakes provide a way of learning. People in control of their lives don't care what you or I think when they make a mistake. They're so busy focusing on their goals when a mistake is made that they look at it as a lesson in what to do differently next time. I had to remember that when I first began doing public workshops. For a number of years I did workshops only when I was invited by an organization or company. It was pretty safe: the participants were "built in" as were the location and training materials. All I had to do was show up.

I was getting tired of not knowing when the next "sale" would be, so I decided to conduct a series of five public workshops in Southern California. I hired someone to help me, designed the program, rented the conference facilities at large hotels, printed 10,000 brochures and sent them out to a mailing list I purchased from New York. All I needed was 50 responses in order to break even and 100 to make some money.

A month after the mailing I had only seven responses and I was in a panic. I thought I had failed miserably. I had done everything I had thought was right and couldn't figure out what had gone wrong. I became immobilized. When a friend called to ask how it was going, I broke down and cried. I felt like a failure. After several days of this, I did some self-talk. I told myself that I had made the right decisions at each moment, but now I needed more information. I began talking to people about how I might improve attendance. With this, things turned around. The feeling of being out of control vanished when I began taking control back. I found several people who had great ideas about how to attract more participants, and the workshops went off without a hitch. Participants appreciated the fact that the meetings were small in size and included personal attention. With each workshop, word got out that it was a great program and by word of mouth the attendance improved.

Through all of this I learned a number of valuable lessons:

1. Keep expenses down and improve enrollment through targeted mailings.
2. I have friends who are there for me when I need them if I allow them to be.
3. I am always in control of my responses to my situation.
4. I prefer working with small groups.
5. There is a need for and interest in my programs.
6. Free advertising is available through newspapers and radio.
7. I made some wonderful contacts at local radio stations.

8. A number of attendees want to utilize my consulting services in their own businesses.
9. I made an audiotape (with one of the women who interviewed me on the radio) that is sold in conjunction with many of my programs.

I could go on, but this will give you an idea of what I mean when I suggest you must make decisions without fear of making mistakes. Had I known then what I know now, I would never have undertaken this endeavor, and I would have missed out on the benefits of the process. Am I sorry I did it? No way. I now know what to do differently next time (and there will be a next time).

Commandment Five

5. *Honor Thy Instincts.*

At some deep level we know what's right for us and what isn't. When we get an internal message, we have the choice of listening to it or rationalizing it away. This is the "Yes, but . . ." we play with ourselves. In order to take control of our lives we must listen to those messages. They carry with them the guideposts by which we make our decisions.

I am now working with a client called Diane who doesn't trust herself enough to honor her instincts. One of her key issues is her inability (or unwillingness) to make a career move. She's in a dead-end job, working with people who are threatened by her ability and talent and she knows, on an intellectual level, she must get out if she is to maintain her dignity and self-respect. Each time she considers making a move, Diane questions whether or not it's the right thing to do. She can find lots of reasons to stay: "I don't want to be a quitter," "Maybe it isn't them after all — it's me" or "What else could I possibly do?" What she won't do is honor her instinct.

We all find pros and cons when making a choice. That's normal. What's debilitating is being immobilized by choices. We instinctively know what's right for us and what's wrong for us. For years others have tried to manipulate us and tell us that we don't know our own minds to the point where even we believe it! Partly this is fear of making mistakes, but also it is honoring ourselves and believing that we can make good choices for ourselves. Remember that others find it easy to decide for you and then you come to believe they do know what's best. One television show from our childhood did much to reinforce the belief that *Father Knows Best.*

Commandment Six

6. *Thou Shalt Feed Thyself As Well As Others.*

As you already know, women are the nurturers and accommodators in society. We learn at an early age how to feed others, literally and figuratively, but no one has ever taught us how to feed ourselves. Our collective depression is a signal that we are starving.

I once heard a story about a rabbi who dies and goes to heaven. Once there he is met by an old man with long white hair and a white beard who ushers him into a room where starving, emaciated people are sitting around a large cauldron filled with piping hot soup. Each person holds a spoon, but the spoon handles are three feet long and the people can't maneuver the spoons into their mouths. Such a waste, thinks the rabbi, all that food and the people are starving.

Then the old man guides the rabbi into a second room. The scene is exactly the same. The people are sitting around a huge cauldron of piping hot food with spoons with three foot handles. The people here, though, are all fat and happy. The difference? The people in the second room have learned that in order to survive they must feed each other.

Commandment Seven

7. *Thou Shalt Not Explain.*

When you are listening to someone talk, what do you do after they have made their point once, twice or even three times? Turn off and tune out. Your patience for listening to someone only lasts so long. When people explain *ad nauseum*, the effect is just the opposite of what they intend. Instead of making their point clear, they diminish their power in the eyes of others.

Effective, deliberate communicators prepare in advance and deliver their message in a cogent fashion. The best communicators I know use an economy of words, secure that they have conveyed the essence of the message and are open to questions from those requiring more detail.

Women, in particular, use far too many words to get points across. The reasons for this vary. Sometimes they are not used to having "the floor" at all, so when they do, they make sure they get their money's worth, but end up losing their message. At other times, they may make their points early, but get no recognition so keep repeating the message, looking for some sign of understanding. Again, this gives an impression of insecurity more than effectively communicating. Or it may simply be that women have had not enough practice of communicating straightforwardly. One woman told me she was so used to repeating to her kids three or four times that when she reentered the workforce, she found herself doing the same with the boss!

Whatever the reason, stop doing it. Make your point, then remain silent. Ask if any clarification is necessary, but don't explain away your reasons. Assume that others will ask questions if they want more information.

Commandment Eight

8. Thou Shalt Not Ask Permission.

This is one important way in which women minimize their sense of personal power. Look around you. When do men ever ask permission to do anything? Men proceed with the assumption of a green light unless told differently. Men inform others of their choices, but don't ask permission to make them.

Women, on the other hand, are afraid of honoring their instincts, making affirmative statements rather than asking questions and making mistakes. So, what do they do? They ask permission. Children in our society are expected to ask permission, but not adult women.

Get yourself into the habit of deciding what it is that you want and then state that in the affirmative. For example, rather than ask, "Would it be okay if I took next Thursday off? My son is graduating from high school," state, "I won't be here next Thursday. My son is graduating from high school." If the boss has a problem with this, you can be sure you'll know about it. If not, you've maintained your own sense of power without infringing on anyone else's. This is what I mean when I say men state their positions and women ask permission. In the same situation in the workplace, men more frequently assert their desires and proceed unless they are told differently.

Commandment Nine

9. Thou Shalt Give Back to the Community a Part of All That Ye Reap.

This Commandment was suggested to me by Barbara Gardner, Director of the Women's Resource Center at the University of California, Riverside. Not too long ago she asked me to be a speaker on the topic of women and control at their annual women's conference. When I asked what she would like me to include, she suggested I remind women that once they have taken control of their lives, they must remember to help others who haven't yet done so.

In corporate America the term "Queen Bee Syndrome" is used to describe what often afflicts women who have been elevated to positions of authority. It suggests that there is only room for one Queen in the hive. Once they have been acknowledged and validated by the system, they assume the characteristics of those in power and begin to behave in similar ways toward those who are not at their level.

Wanting to forget about a painful past is common and understandable. It's seen all the time. Minorities who "make it" leave the ghetto, never to return. The chronically ill "beat the odds" and turn their backs on those who haven't. Children who surpass their parents in material wealth are often embarrassed by their simple upbringing. We would like to close our eyes and erase the memories which are reminders of times and places better left forgotten.

Part of what makes women uniquely women is their working in partnership with the world. Unlike most men who see the world as something to be conquered and made part of their private domain, women generally have the gift of working collaboratively and cooperatively. To ignore this is to lose an essential part of who we are. We cannot turn our backs on those to whom we can be of help. We must not. We have a responsibility to our sisters who may still be bound by invisible chains of fear.

It is imperative that as we grow in understanding and acceptance of our own power and control over our lives, we return to the community a portion of this knowledge. We must share with others our successes and our insights. We are bound together in this world with a responsibility for the welfare of others. This is not to say this responsibility supercedes our own needs (Commandment Six), but rather is complementary to them. For there is a synergy to helping others in our community. We can make a difference in the lives of others that multiplies exponentially.

Commandment Ten

10. Visualize Power.

For the longest time I kept telling myself that when I completed my doctorate, I would reward myself with the car of my dreams. As the defending of my dissertation approached, I found myself with more time to look for this car. I was disappointed to learn how expensive the car was and realized it might be a long time before I could actually afford it.

One day I put a brochure featuring a picture of my "dream car" on the refrigerator. I kept thinking that maybe I would be able to locate one in my price range, even if it was used. For the next several months I continued to visit dealerships looking for my car. I test-drove all colors, styles and features. As the defense date drew closer, I resigned myself to not driving a new car to campus that day. Then I saw one advertised at a dealership for about 35% less than the normal cost.

The car was new, but a demo that people test drive and the dealership loans to its employees. It had low mileage and more features than I ever thought I could afford. That was the car I drove to my dissertation defense. That, in and of itself, is not so amazing. But what I soon realized was that the car on the refrigerator was the exact car that I had purchased. The color of the interior and exterior was the same, the extra features were the same and the style was the same. It *was* the car on the refrigerator!

Prior to this experience my friend Sandra had been talking to me for some time about creative visualization. She spoke of amazing things that could happen to those who dared to visualize what they wanted in their lives. From that point on Sandra didn't have to sell me. I became a true believer. As I learned more about it, I came to understand what a powerful tool it could be to me personally and in my work as a psychotherapist.

Commandment Ten suggests that you must *begin to see yourself as a powerful person*. If you have been out of touch with your power your entire life, you don't know what power feels like. "How will I know when I am becoming powerful?" is the question I am often asked by clients. Women often have no sense of their power, no baseline of understanding of what it means to be powerful.

Types Of Power

I recently sat in on a workshop given by Bruce Gillespie from ARCO Oil & Gas Company. During the workshop Bruce told participants to "pick their power." By that he meant there are different ways to exhibit your power and you can choose and visualize which kind you want to achieve and perfect. Let me try to paraphrase Bruce's descriptions of the kinds of power available to you:

1. *Coercive Power.* Whenever you are in a situation where you force your will on others, then you are exercising coercive power. Usually there is a threat implied toward failure to recognize someone using this type of power. Parents frequently use coercive power with children. Either the child does what you ask or they are punished. Similarly in work situations, either you do what the boss requests or you are fired. Coercive power doesn't always have to be seen as negative and threatening, however. If I am in a burning building and you coerce me into vacating it against my will, thus saving my life, I might not necessarily view your exercising coercive power as negative. The problem with coercive power is that it only lasts so long. Children grow up, employees quit or wives leave their husbands. One suggestion for successfully using this kind of power is to allow others to select their own punishment. What may be punishment for you may not be punishment for someone else.

2. *Legitimate Power.* Another way of looking at this kind of power is "position power." By virtue of my position, I am endowed with a legitimate source of power. Insecure people continually remind others of their legitimate power, such as the boss who keeps reminding us of this fact or the parent who towers over the child. More secure people just use it naturally when they give instructions, a work assignment, make a request or bargain with a vendor.

3. *Reward Power.* The horse that is coaxed along with the carrot is being influenced by reward power. Whenever I say I'll give you something to make you do what I want, I am using reward power. Every time I collect my consulting fee, I am being influenced by reward power. To use reward power effectively, three things must be present: the reward level must be commensurate with the act, the reward must be specific and it must be genuine. One of the best forms of reward power is praise. The fastest way to assure an act will be repeated is to praise the actor.

Some of the most powerful people in business are confident enough to praise others, thereby securing their trust and loyalty.

4. Expert Power. When you learn more than others in a field and they have to come to you for answers and guidance, then you are using expert power. There are two primary problems with using this type of power: (1) it takes time away from you each time you have to stop and answer questions and (2) you must always take the time to use it carefully so you don't lose the respect you have gained as an "expert."

Women working inside the home who know where to find everything belonging to everyone in the household know exactly what I mean by expert power. Like the previous forms of power, it has its advantages and disadvantages. Experts are powerful in that they get people to rely on them, but the question to ask yourself is, do you really want people running to you every time they need something? If you feel insecure about your expertise in a particular area and this is holding you back in any way, then by all means do whatever is necessary for you to gain the confidence you need to feel like an expert.

5. Referent Power. John F. Kennedy, Ronald Reagan, Adolph Hitler, Golda Meir, Martin Luther King and Mae West are examples of referent power. People who are charismatic are said to be using referent power. It has been suggested that you can develop this kind of power but take care in making such a choice. People tend to vacillate between loving and hating this type of powerful person. These people are inspiring, but like moths attracted to a flame, other people can get burned if they get too close.

Take the time before you go to sleep or before you get out of bed in the morning, and imagine what kind of power you would like to use and what it would be like to be powerful. How would it feel? What would it mean for you? Ask yourself, "What would I be doing today if I were in touch with my power?" Begin to visualize your strength and your behaviors as you act in a powerful way.

If you have difficulty doing this, go back to the relaxation exercise described in Chapter Four. Remember, visualizing power means having control over your life. With each breath that you take during the exercise, be conscious of inhaling a wave of positive energy . As you exhale, feel a calm sense of power filling your limbs. Do this as many times as necessary until you begin to envision the kind of power required for making the changes that will give you control of your life.

EXERCISE:

You are the only one who knows what's holding you back. What is it that you must change in order to take back control of your life? Does "I shalt not give my power away to my mother" ring true? How about "I shalt complete my education"? Maybe "I shalt have more fun" is on your list. Whatever your additional commandments are, write them down here. Think about what would make you feel more powerful and in control and write a commandment for it.

Commandment Eleven

_____

_____

Commandment Twelve

_____

_____

Commandment Thirteen

_____

_____

Commandment Fourteen

8
Putting It All Together

*The journey of a thousand miles
begins with a single step.*

Lao-Tzu

Give yourself credit. Purchasing this book was a good step toward taking back control of your life. Then by completing all of the exercises, you have taken several more steps. If you're still with me, I give you a lot of credit. The things that I have asked you to think about haven't been easy. I've challenged you to question your belief system and the systems of those around you. What do you do now? Turn ideas and feelings into action. The things that have been discussed so far will be of no value to you unless you use them to make a change in your life.

The majority of this last chapter will be written by you. It has to be. I've shared with you ways in which anger is turned into depression, why this happens, what gets in the way of being angry and methods to express your anger and regain control of your life. Now it's up to you. I can't take the steps that will help you reach your personal goals and dreams. Only you can do that. So, in this chapter I ask you to complete an action plan. By going through the steps, you will leave this book with a clearer understanding of how you express your depression and your anger, and what you must do to take back control of your life.

As you complete the plan, you may want to go back and review some of your previous responses to earlier questionnaires and checklists. Don't labor over any one item; your spontaneous response will be an honest reflection of your feelings. If you have difficulty with any particular item, skip it and go back later. If you still have a problem, then you may want to think about why. The inability to answer a question can provide as much insight for you as the answer itself. By completing this last step and committing to action, you will be in a better position to make the changes necessary to find your anger and lose your depression.

Personal Action Plan
For Taking Control Of My Life

1. The main thing I learned about my depression as a result of reading this book:

   _____

   _____

   _____ .

2. The ways in which I express or exhibit my depression are:

   _____

_____

_____ .

3. Some of the key things that I learned about how others contribute to my depression that I never realized before include:

_____

_____

_____ .

4. When I think about depression being related to anger, what I realize contributes most to my being depressed is my anger over:

_____

_____

_____ .

5. In my family anger was expressed by:

_____

_____

_____ .

6. The ways in which I hide my anger are:

_____

_____

_____ .

7. My biggest fear about expressing my anger is:

_____

_____

_____ .

8. The situation that makes me most angry is:

_____

_____

_____ .

9. In the short term, I will take the following steps to deal with this situation by:

_____

_____

_____.

10. In the long term, I will take the following steps to deal with this situation by:

_____

_____

_____.

11. The person who makes me the most angry is:

_____

_____

_____.

12. The things this person does (or has done) to make me angry include:

_____

_____

_____.

13. If I could say anything to this person, it would be:

_____

_____

_____.

14. What stops me from saying these things is:

_____

_____

_____.

15. To overcome this I will:

_____

_____

_____.

16. The things that depress me about my relationships with others are:

_____

_____

_____.

17. In order to have better relationships with others, I will:

_____

_____

_____.

18. The biggest obstacle to having more control over my life is:

_____

_____

_____.

19. In order to overcome this obstacle I must:

_____

_____

_____.

20. Beginning today, I commit to doing the following things to gain more personal power and control:

_____

_____

_____.

21. At work I would like to have more control over:

_____

_____

_____.

22. My biggest obstacle to gaining that control is:

_____

_____

_____.

23. In the short term, I will do the following things to gain more control at work:

_____

_____

_____.

24. In the long term, I will do the following things to gain more control at work:

_____

_____

_____.

25. The three self-messages I will give myself on a daily basis about achieving personal satisfaction and fulfillment are:

A. _____.

B. _____.

C. _____.

I'm going to leave you now to your thoughts and feelings. I appreciate the work we have done together. If you are still with me at this point, I already know something about you even though I may never have met you personally. I know that you are powerful enough to confront even the most difficult issues. You want your life to change, and I know that you are capable of making that change. Please continue on your journey, using whatever resources are available to you. Use safe people to give you feedback about how you are doing. Use books and workshops to learn more. Use therapy as a means of moving further and deeper. Most of all, use your own intuition and trust that it is right. It is yours. It is in your awareness for a reason. You don't need proof or have to explain your feelings. The fact that the feelings exist is reason enough to trust and listen to them. I wish you luck and, even more, I wish that you achieve the dreams that others tell you are impossible.

BIBLIOGRAPHY

Adler, A.: Individual Psychology. In Murchison (Ed.), **Psychologies of 1930.** Clark University Press, New York, 1930.

American Psychiatric Association DSM-III: Diagnostic and Statistical Manual of Mental Disorders (Third Edition). Washington, D.C., 1980.

Baker Miller, J.: **Toward A New Psychology of Women.** Beacon Press, Boston, 1976.

Bierig, S.: **Transforming The Co-dependent Woman.** Health Communications, Deerfield Beach, Florida, 1991.

Capra, F.: **The Turning Point.** Bantam Books, New York, 1983.

Cohen, L.: "The Sisters of Mercy." Song by Judy Collins, Elektra Records.

Einstein, A.: Letter to Dr. M. I. Cohen, in Bertrand Russell affair, *New York World Telegram,* March 19, 1940.

Frankl, V.: **The Will To Meaning.** The New American Library, New York, 1969.

Freud, A.: The Conceptual Lines of Development. In **The Psychoanalytic Study of the Child.** Volume 18. International Universities Press, New York, 1963.

Morrow Lindbergh, A.: **Gift from the Sea.** Vintage Books, New York, 1965.

Piercy, M.: **To Be of Use.** Doubleday, New York, 1973.

Stephens, B.: In conversation, Los Angeles, November, 1987.

Weissman, M.: As quoted in Ihsan Al-Issa (Ed.), **Gender and Psychopathology.** Academic Press, Inc., New York, 1982.

Wilson Schaef, A.: **Women's Reality.** Winston Press, Minneapolis, 1981.

Wood Wetzel, J.: **Clinical Handbook of Depression.** Gardner Press, New York, 1984.